BORN
TOO
SOON

BORN TOO SOON

SUE ENGELMAN

Horizon Books
Beaverlodge, Alberta Canada
Cathedral City, California

Horizon Books
are published by
Horizon House Publishers
Box 600
Beaverlodge, AB TOH OCO Canada
Drawer AA, Cathedral City, CA 92234

Printed in the United States

Table of Contents

1
Number Four On The Way

Teeming with mixed emotions and physically exhausted, I asked, "What is it?"

"It's a boy!" my husband exclaimed. Phil's eyes rounded with wonder.

Mom cautiously peeked into the bed as if her looking might harm this fragile baby. "Oh Sue, he's so tiny."

As the midwife laid the warm, wet Michael Tim on my chest, a great sense of peace flooded my soul. "He's finally here," I sighed. My eyes scanned his form. His minute nose resembled Phil's—cute little point to it, slightly upturned.

Michael's story had begun five and a half months before.

I'll never forget the first day I suspected I was pregnant with our fourth child. I was frying eggs. The breakfast aromas normally made my taste buds tingle. Often I'd snatch little bites as I made the family meal. But this day, even the thought of crackling bacon made my stomach roll. I could almost feel the grease hit my belly. The special moment when a woman first realizes she may have a secret "within" is always thrilling. My first thought that morning was, "Oh no, I hope it's not the flu," and then, "I wonder...am I expecting?"

I've often thought how nice it would be to wake up

one day and discover I was three months pregnant. But it's never been like that for me. It seems like two weeks after conception, almost on the dot, I'm already experiencing the effects. How romantic it would be if I could inform my husband of our news over a candlelight dinner, you know, the way you always see it done in the movies—Phil's handsome face enhanced by the glow of the candles, his blue eyes deepening as we silently partake of a scrumptious gourmet meal and gaze at each other lovingly. Of course I'd be wearing my prettiest blue dress, with my make-up and hair in carefully studied place. Then that special magnetism would draw us closer. I would lean over to kiss Phil's moustached mouth and whisper, "Guess what, honey? I'm going to have a baby!" His dimpled smile would reveal his evenly placed teeth and he'd reply, "Really? That's wonderful!"

But this time I just couldn't keep the secret that long. Phil knew the moment I suspected. My already pale complexion turned to a sickly white pallor and my sense of smell was so heightened that all kinds of aromas nauseated me. Hamburger grease and cigarette smoke reached out and turned my stomach into knots. Stepping from the shower, I'd spritz on my favorite cologne and suddenly my nose and stomach would rebel. What usually smelled pleasantly sweet turned to cotton-candy saccharin.

As time wore on, the all too familiar symptoms continued to mount. "Fuzzy head" syndrome was the first signal. My head felt as if it were encased in cotton. My sense of balance was off. My brain seemed like it could float out into space any moment. I often wondered if drug addicts felt this way. If I looked at a distant object and then turned to focus on something else, my eyes dizzily lagged behind.

Phil and I very "discreetly" told a circle of about

ten people our private news. We never could keep this secret very well. On November 10th, I went to a local clinic and the pregnancy test confirmed our suspicions. Engelman number four was definitely on the way.

I could hardly believe I was pregnant. It seemed too good to be true. The timing was just right. Everything was ticking according to plan.

Events in my life seemed to follow this pattern again and again. Things I really wanted the most I got eventually. I wonder if my mother, Alma, felt that way the day she gave me birth. It was November 3, 1951 in South Bend, Indiana. I think I was born scheming. I had to be a schemer with four brothers. I was smack in the middle with two older and two younger. The nearest town of Teegarden had a bulging population of approximately one hundred. My desires were not hard to satisfy back then. Our life was simple. Dad worked in both construction and farming, trying to feed our hungry family. We had a nice garden and lots of land around for all of us kids to run, to roam and in the winter to ice skate on.

Our family of seven moved to Florida when I was thirteen. It was just what I wanted. But what an adjustment! On my first day of school, I was laughed down because I wore white anklets. Hey, I didn't know that wasn't cool.

I adapted quickly though. I even learned how to answer, "Yes, Ma'am," and "No, Sir," though it seemed rudely formal to me. Kids called me "Pinky" because I wore pink bows.

I made friends slowly. It was easier for me to observe people first. I was your typical goody-goody who genuinely leaned toward the more wholesome side. I kept my eyes on the nice girls and boys. They were the kids I copied. Somehow I managed to get all the classes I wanted. My favorite teachers fell into place.

9

Even my closest friends ended up in the same classes with me. It sort of spooked me how things seemed to go so well for me all the time. I didn't deserve any of this so I chalked it up to luck. Good grades came with each report card. My boyfriend was cute. I even made cheerleading.

Things in Pompano Beach were even nicer. I was a majorette for a while though I was awfully clumsy. I never could do a front spin for fear the baton would crack my head.

Junior high was fun. More things went my way. School seemed easier. My circle of friends grew. High school brought more cheerleading, more friends. I dated a popular football player and became assistant editor of our school newspaper. All the time I kept thinking, "How can all this happen to me?" My friends never realized how insecure I was. I was kind of shy and believed people wouldn't like me if they knew what I was really like, so I didn't open up very often.

Some nagging spiritual questions haunted me. Though people didn't see it, I was a deeply frightened girl. Even at sixteen I still cried myself to sleep because of fears about death. My desire to know what the truth really was about God and life after death climaxed at a youth meeting. There I discovered God was not an angry ogre out to get me and take away my fun. He loved me and sent His Son Jesus to die for me. It was hard for me to believe heaven was a free gift. A friend showed me Ephesians 2:8,9: "For by grace are ye saved through faith and that not of yourselves. It is the gift of God, not of works lest any man should boast." All my good works meant nothing to God if I came on my own merit. I had to come through Jesus Christ alone because He alone was perfect and sinless. Only He could pay for my sins. When He died on the cross He died for me. That night I accepted Christ as my personal Savior. It was the first peaceful night's sleep I'd had in years.

I realized then what I thought of as luck was God's providence working in my life. My fears slowly dissolved as I gave myself completely to His control. He had a plan for me and was weaving the pattern. My reputation as a goody-goody grew. In my junior year, I met a skinny, yet handsome boy named Phil. He had this great smile and innocent boyish look. His brown hair was full with touches of golden streaks that accented his hazel blue eyes. He sang in a contemporary Christian music group and had such a beautiful voice. He seemed to have a zeal for the Lord and that attracted me even more. I quit dating other guys at school. I wanted someone who had a depth to them that came from God. My insecurities made it hard for me to believe Phil would ever like me. After two years of admiring each other from afar, he finally asked me out. I knew he'd probably drop me once he found out the real me. Our first date was unbelievably romantic. I wanted to spend my life with this man. Incredibly he felt the same way. Three months later, we became secretly engaged and a year later, on June 12th, 1971, we got married.

Phil struggled through Bible College. My health deteriorated. Leg pain plagued me for months. The doctors hadn't been able to help. I was finally forced to quit work. Bills were high and food was low, but God always managed to supply our needs. Eventually I got relief through the skills of the right doctor, but more illness plagued me. When Phil finally graduated, we headed off for Winter Haven, Florida where we spent two years. My health problems subsided. Holly and David were born. Life seemed blissfully problem free. We moved to St. Petersburg, where Phil served as a youth pastor. When his father retired from the ministry, the church surprisingly voted Phil to be his successor at the young age of twenty-six. We were enjoying the ministry. Life was good. Things were going according to plan.

We were your typical family. One girl and one boy. Three years later, we decided we didn't want to stop with just two children. Finally after three more years, Jonathan, our third child was born. It was a dream. He was a perfect kid, slept long, ate a lot, and hardly ever cried. As Jonathan grew he brought so much joy we wanted one more, and now number four was on the way. I was ecstatic.

That evening in prayer, Phil and I gave the baby to the Lord for whatever use He intended and prayed for his future. Following our usual pattern, we began to proclaim our happy news to everyone. Phil made our announcement officially that next Sunday in church. When you are in the pastorate, a lot of things become sermon material!

Although many people were happy, I think they were also surprised that we were having number four so soon after thirteen-month-old Jonathan. I'm sure most people just assumed he was an "accident" or that we were crazy. With raised eyebrows, a smiling woman asked, "Accidents do happen, don't they?"

"Oh this was no accident," I responded. "The car's still in great shape. No, seriously, we just love kids." Quite frankly, our son Jonathan had been such a fun, easy-going baby that I was thinking more and more that I might like to have six children! Little did I know the significance of that thought.

Being a pastor's wife was anything but boring— midnight phone calls, crisis counseling, and a seemingly revolving front door made our lives happy, exciting, but sometimes touched by heartache and sorrow. Still, nothing compares with the awesome and life-changing experience of a child being knit in the womb.

I'll never forget the night Phil and I were awakened by a phone call at 1 a.m. "Phil, Stephanie's dead! I found her in her crib with a little blood trickling from her nose. She wasn't breathing and I tried to revive her, but...." The father's voice trailed off in despair. Phil rushed to their home to give whatever comfort he could.

Several other women in our church had experienced multiple miscarriages and yet another friend lost her daughter when she was born with no kidneys. All this within a two year period. Sometimes I wondered if it wasn't my turn this time. But as quickly as these thoughts entered, I swiftly shoved them out of my mind. After all, it had never happened to me before. Why would it this time? My anticipation about our new child grew. The nagging doubts just faded away.

Life began to take on a whole new perspective. Suddenly, my diet underwent strict scrutiny and I had a new zeal to eat properly. Breads, sweets, and junk food were the first to go. Fresh fruits, vegetables and wholegrains replaced the junk. I had been jogging approximately three miles three times a week for a year, so I decided I would continue on with my normal exercise routine for at least five months into the pregnancy. "Are you sure you should do that?" my well-meaning friends would ask. "Won't all that bobbing up and down hurt the baby?"

"It's fine, really," I would assure them. "Lynne, my midwife, told me one of her patients jogged until she was nine months along." A startled expression would follow and most tried not to show they weren't convinced.

I reassessed my wardrobe and decided I would have to get the sewing machine out from under the dust cover and create some new maternity outfits. My whole world, every waking moment, included the baby. Engelman number four was becoming an increasingly important part of my life. We even decided the names. Boy, Michael Tim Engelman—named after my brother, Phil's cousin and Phil's brother, or girl, Heather Renee, because our daughter Holly liked the name Heather and Renee was after my mother. We later decided on Abigail Lynne—Lynne, after our midwife, and Abigail because a man in the church suggested the name and we liked it. After all, Abigail was a Bible character we greatly admired.

I very dutifully made a doctor's appointment to confirm that everything was all right. Lynne Dollar knew we were planning another child and was not surprised by my visit. She also confirmed the pregnancy. Prompted by a guilty conscience, I sheepishly asked, "Are you sure it's all right for me to continue my jogging? People are asking questions."

She smiled, knowing I had a phobia about trying to please all the people in the congregation. "If you feel good, I see no reason why you should stop. You've been doing this for a long time now so your body is already used to it. I'll try to drum up some articles on the subject if you want. I thought I saw one the other day in a medical magazine. They haven't done much research on pregnancy and jogging, but I'll give you what I have."

"Thanks," I sighed, "it would make me feel better." I left the office engulfed in peace.

I was experiencing some nausea but not severe. The main problem I noticed was my mood swings. Some days I was so irritable I had trouble controlling my anger. Waves of depression and doubt for seemingly no reason produced tears at the drop of a hat. I had to constantly lean on God's Word and Phil's patience to help me through those moments. I continued my jogging three times a week although it felt like lead weights were tied to my legs.

2
"This Baby's Not A Keeper"

On the evening of November 16, I was sitting quietly in our den working on some cross stitch. Christmas would be coming soon. Phil and I decided we would make our gifts this year. Each evening after the kids were in bed we would sit down and share some blissful quiet together—Phil, with his newly-found hobby, woodcarving, and me with my cross stitch. I settled down in my chair to begin the pattern when I realized I didn't have everything I needed. As I got up, I felt a strange rushing sensation and realized I was bleeding. Too shocked to believe it was true, I rushed to the bathroom. "Phil!" I shouted. "Call the midwife!"

Phil ran back where I was, disbelief and shock widening his eyes. "What's wrong? Are you losing the baby? This isn't normal, is it?" His rapid-fire questions irritated me.

"Please, just get Lynne!" I retorted sharply. He jumbled through the phone numbers and dialed.

Thoughts raced through my mind. "Am I losing the baby? Maybe I shouldn't have gone jogging yesterday. Was I doing something wrong?" I laid down on our bed and propped my feet up. Fear pushed a button inside that started my legs shaking. I was scared. I didn't want to lose the baby. Just the thought of it produced tears.

As we waited for Lynne's return call, we talked. Phil

could see my fear gradually turning to hysteria so he spoke soothingly. "I'm sure you're fine, Honey. The Lord knows. He'll watch over us."

"Honey, I realize that just as I trusted in Jesus Christ for my salvation, now I've got to trust Him to know what He's doing in my life with our child. After all, we already gave this baby to the Lord. Wasn't He just as concerned as we were, or more, for this life?" The more we talked, the more God's peace took hold and covered me like a blanket.

Soon Ann Hager, the other midwife at the clinic, called. Still sniffling, I explained everything to her.

"Sue, there's probably no reason for alarm. Many women do bleed for various reasons especially during the earlier months. I know you must be frightened. Many women have expressed how terrifying it is to have this happen."

I replied, "Well, you know, Phil and I have been talking about this. We realize this baby is God's and has been from the moment of conception. He knows what He's doing and if it's His will for this baby to survive He'll let everything be all right."

Our conversation ended with Ann telling me to come down to the clinic in the morning. They could check me over then. Once again, I pushed the doubts and fears from my mind and clung to the promises I knew were true.

The next morning I got up early and made plans to go to the clinic. Phoning our sweet adopted grandmother, Alice O'Connor, I asked her if she would take me. I was still feeling a little weak. The bleeding was not heavy but it had continued.

The exam showed that my uterus was swollen, but everything seemed to be all right. They decided to do an ultrasound. Little did I know this would be the first in a string of many.

I had never had an ultrasound before so the procedure was explained. I was told to drink three huge glasses of water. I've never hated water, but drinking that much at one time was sickening. My queasy, empty stomach didn't take too well to the cold water. My arms and soon my legs began to tremble. Embarrassed that people in the waiting room might see me, I huddled down in the chair. Using all my strength I tried in vain to calm the shaking.

A pretty red-haired freckle-faced nurse called me to the ultrasound room. I lay down on a bed next to a strange machine that looked like a TV screen and a typewriter combined. I asked the fresh-faced girl, "Why can't I quit shaking?"

"I think it's the cold water," she smiled. "Most of the girls shake. Here, let me give you another sheet. My name is Jessie, and I'll be doing your ultrasound today. This is all done with sound waves and we should be able to get a picture of your baby." She squirted some ice cold jelly on my abdomen. I jumped. "I'm sorry," Jessie apologized. "I wish this stuff wasn't so cold. Doesn't help you much does it?" Next, she rubbed a smooth flat instrument over the jelly on my stomach. It transmitted the picture.

Jessie soon called in Lynne, the midwife, and they began to explain what they were seeing. They showed me a picture of what a normal four to six week pregnancy would look like. It was similar to a pear-shaped balloon with a little ball inside it. So far, all they could see in my case was a blood-filled uterus. As the picture became clearer they also saw a sac with a little ball in it, but it looked as though it had collapsed. As we all continued to watch the picture on the screen, I cried, "I'm bleeding again."

"We know," Lynne said, "we can see it on the screen." A moment of silence followed. "You can change now, Sue, and come back to the examining room. We'd also like a urine sample before you come. One of the doctors will want to check you out and then we'll talk to you some more."

I rushed into the bathroom. "What in the world is going on?" I was still very confused by all that was happening. My thoughts scattered. "Can't tell what that crazy sonogram shows. I'm not used to seeing that. I don't know what to look for. I don't like all this mystery. I'm so scared."

As I slipped on my clothes and walked back to the examining room, my emotions were running wild. I wouldn't allow myself to believe that I was losing the baby and every time the thought came, I pushed it aside.

"You're okay, Sue," Lynne said, touching my shoulder as she guided me down the hall. "You've had three normal pregnancies. So you have a little bleeding. Lots of women bleed a little in the early months." In a fog, I slowly wandered into the examining room. Lynne exited, closing the white door behind her. I wondered, "Is she just trying to calm me down? Is she telling me the truth?"

One of the doctors from the clinic briskly opened the door and entered, accompanied by Lynne. His white coat matched his graying hair. He looked cold and official. My body tensed. I didn't like the solemn looks on their faces. I wished Phil was there. If only I had known this visit would be so serious. The doctor examined me and confirmed I had not begun to dilate and the cervix was still tight and closed. "Oh good," I thought, "maybe everything is all right after all."

Interrupting my optimistic thoughts he began to speak. He grabbed my hand and patted it. It seemed like a patronizing gesture and it didn't fit his vacant emotions.

"Well, Sue, from all that I've seen on the sonogram pictures and your exam, I would say, let's face it, this baby's not a keeper. Most women have a sac and you can even see a little heart beating in it. Yours looked as though it had collapsed. This is how most pregnancies look when they're about to abort. I'm sorry."

I tried to control myself. My lips quivered. The moment he uttered those words, "pregnancy about to abort" I froze. I couldn't believe what I was hearing. His blue eyes darted around the room, looking everywhere but at me. His words lacked any emotion. "If you haven't already lost the baby, you are about to. All indications seem to point to this. Your pregnancy test just came out negative and things just don't look good from here on out. You will probably miscarry in the next couple of days. Now, you have a couple of options. You can let your body continue to do what it is doing and abort the baby on your own. It could take three to five days. It would be a tiring and uncomfortable experience, or you can let us put you into the hospital now, give you a D and C and you can get on with living."

I began to cry. This whole macabre scene lacked reality. Had I just been told I lost my baby? I was shocked. Why did this doctor make me feel it was silly to cry? I was also angered at his feeble attempt to understand how I felt. His "I'm sorry" seemed like an added afterthought of politeness. "This baby's not a keeper" rang in my ears. Didn't he know he was talking about my child, not a piece of tissue you throw away? Lynne stood silent through the whole conversation.

I swallowed hard, but I knew instantly what my choice was. I didn't have to think about it. "Well, I feel very strongly about the life of this baby. If God wants to take it, then it would be best for Him to do it in His own timing and not mine. Is there any danger to me physically in allowing this to happen?"

"We'd have to keep a close eye on you to make sure you're not hemorraging or becoming infected. We'll need to see you in a couple of days." He turned his solemn face directly toward me instead of the wall. "I'm sorry things turned out this way." With that he walked out of the room.

"I'm sorry, Sue." Lynne spoke compassionately. "I wish it wasn't going this way for you. We respect your wishes and we won't force the D and C but be real careful, okay?" Her small hand lightly touched my shoulder. "Are you okay?" she asked.

"Yes," I answered tearfully, but all I wanted to do was cry.

As I changed my clothes in the sterile white booth, I started sorting out all that just transpired. Had I really lost the baby, or was it still there? Was I pregnant or not? If I still had the baby, what would it be like to miscarry? Grotesque pictures of baby pieces haunted me. Would I be in pain? Questions continued to flood my soul. The more I thought, the more questions arose. Tears began to flow. This whole day was so hard to comprehend. I had to get myself back home and discuss all this with Phil. I stepped out of the room into the hallway.

I still can't remember why I was supposed to go to the lab room and wait. I think they were going to poke my finger and get a blood count. Seated uncomfortably on a little stool by the doorway, I waited in silence for the nurse to come by and finish her task. Nurses were milling around, busy in their routines. I was so exhausted I couldn't even manage a polite smile. Busyness annoyed me. How could life continue so normally when I was experiencing such turmoil? A woman stepped in the room from the opposite doorway. She looked like she was five months along, glowing, smiling, blissfully unaware of all the tragic things I had just been told.

Wham! Like a cold, heavy door shutting in my face I realized that I might never get to her stage. In fact, I might not even be pregnant now! That weighty door jerked me into life's harsh realities. Emotion began to develop like a volcano in my soul. Building, building, its waves were no longer under my control. Like the gentle rain before a storm, tears began to trickle down my face. My heart felt like it was breaking. I gasped for breath. I had never felt such grief.

Lynne walked into the room. She grabbed my hand and put her arm around me to help me off the stool. "The least I can do is give you a room to cry in," she said. "You don't have to be out here in front of everyone." I needed to be shielded from curious stares. She ushered me into a vacant doctor's office. I plopped on the couch as the volcano released it's fury. The storm broke. I could hardly catch my breath between sobs.

"Yes, we get attached to our little ones very early, don't we?" Lynne tenderly asked. I nodded tearfully. She left me after giving an empathetic hug and a box of tissues.

I cried a while longer and then tried to gather my strength. I needed to go out to the reception desk and make an appointment for Friday the nineteenth. Sheer determination forced my body to comply and to walk down the hall. The receptionist gave a look of concern, her brown eyes edged in tenderness. I signaled to Grandma and she came to meet me. Again, I felt the volcano's force. I wanted to get out of that office as quickly as I could before I exploded. As the office door shut behind me, I once again unleashed the tears.

Poor Grandma. If the situation hadn't been so serious, it would've been almost funny. I had no time to tell her anything. She just silently followed two steps behind her pale, practically hysterical granddaughter. When we reached the car, she whispered, "No baby?" As I opened the door I laughed and cried at the same time. How I loved her for her patience in not demanding an earlier explanation. Slowly I told her the sad verdict. She was losing or had already lost a grandchild.

"Oh," she answered, her word not speaking the inward groan she felt.

When we arrived home Grandma insisted that she stay with me a while. I assured her I would be all right and that I needed to be alone. She hugged me and reluctantly left. By this time I had gathered some of my thoughts and felt a compelling urge to share my report. I knew Phil would be home soon. He was picking up a friend at the airport. The silence in the house was deafening. I needed to talk to someone so I called one of my friends and tearfully related the whole story. The awful events of the day now seemed more real. As I hung up the phone Phil walked in the door. Our eyes met.

He saw my tear-stained face and rushed to pull me into his arms with a reassuring hug. Stroking my hair, he held me there and we shared a loving silence.

3
Pregnant or Not?

The next few days were emotion-packed as the realities of the situation became more and more evident. I struggled to find clothes I could fit into that weren't maternity. All my pants were too tight and my dresses had unforgiving waistlines. It was confusing not knowing whether I was still pregnant or not. Should I be relieved? Was it all over? Could I put a name to what I was feeling? Was it grief? I felt like a time bomb waiting to explode. Women in the church who had miscarriages began to call and share their stories. I was amazed at how many women had lost a child. I was beginning to realize miscarriage was an untalked about subject. It seemed cloaked in mystery and I feared the unknown. I was afraid to ask for gruesome details, yet I needed to. And worst of all, was I or wasn't I?

I mentally prepared myself for the onslaught of comments and loving advice I knew we'd receive. I'd been told by others how most people just don't know what to say when things like this happen, but our congregation was wonderful. The phone began to ring off the hook. Most of the time Phil answered. I felt too physically and emotionally weak to deal with all the calls. Many people sent cards and good, home-cooked meals began to pour through our doors. Two couples sent flowers. The minute I saw them I cried. I was happy someone else recognized a loss in our family. Oh how their bright colors cheered me. All in all we were enveloped in love. I was beginning to let myself believe I'd lost the baby.

Of course, you always have those who try to comfort yet just don't have the right words. Only a few people said, "Oh well, you're young. You can have others," or "Well, at least be thankful it happened now instead of later." I was truly learning the value of silence. I just couldn't explain to them why this experience hurt so very much.

One woman calmly related, "I don't know why but I have a real inner peace about this whole situation. I'm not even worried." The lilt in her voice twisted my stomach. "I know God's going to work it all out."

I loved that lady dearly but I felt the reason she had such peace was because she wasn't in my shoes. She didn't know what I knew. My baby's life hadn't ebbed inside her, so she couldn't feel my emptiness. I knew she wasn't trying to come across as compassionless. It was her way of trying to encourage me. Yet I needed someone to cry with me and not offer pat answers. Her "peace of God" came across to me as an unintentional inability to empathize. All I wanted was someone to listen to me, to be quiet, to give hugs. The verses and assurances had their time and place, just not now. I managed a weak smile, nodded and let the issue drop.

Later I shared with her my thoughts about her comment. One thing I was learning from all this was that I needed to be more honest with people, to share in love what comforts and what doesn't. Yes, I did have God's peace, yet in that peace I was physically going through grief and pain and I desperately wanted people to share some of that with me. Sometimes the most comforting words people offered were in the form of complete silence. Just a tender look in their eyes, the squeeze of my hand. It was all I needed, for in that I knew they were sharing some of my pain.

I guess I never really knew that women who had miscarriages grieved. Whenever I heard someone had a miscarriage, I thought, "Oh, that's too bad." That was the extent of my concern. In the world we live in today so many try to de-emphasize the importance of a life so young or even deny there is a life. I read Psalm 139:13-24 over and over and was comforted especially by verse 16: "Your eyes saw my unformed body. All the days ordained for me were written in your book." God considered this a life from the moment of conception and He knew exactly how long and how many days this child would live. This baby was very important to me even though I had only known of his presence for four short weeks.

The days wore on. I spotted a little yet I never experienced any cramping or other symptoms. Weakness and nausea were present. I still felt pregnant. Had I really lost the baby? I was beginning to think I hadn't.

I became more and more hopeful. I had an idea. Friday enroute to my appointment I would take a morning catch of urine to a local clinic to see if the pregnancy test was positive. Knowing it might be a hard visit, Phil accompanied me to the doctor's office. First stop was the clinic. My thoughts retrogressed to the day I was first told of this pregnancy. When the test came out positive I smiled and turned to my little son Jonathan. "I hope this will be your baby sister."

"Yes," the woman grinned. "That would be nice. One of each."

"Oh, I have two others at home, a boy and a girl," I replied. I'll never forget her look. She must have thought I was the craziest woman she'd met or else terribly irresponsible for overpopulating the world. This same clinic also performed abortions and that grieved me. "What irony," I thought. "Here is a place giving information and service that provides both joy and tragedy in the same day."

But today, November nineteenth, my thoughts were so different. What would I do if this test was negative? What if it was positive? Would that mean that I was still pregnant?

"Sue," the woman behind the counter called. "Have you been experiencing symptoms of pregnancy?"

"Yes," I answered.

"Your test came out positive." I told her of my bleeding and asked if it was possible for some of the hormones to still be present in my body to make my test show positive even if I wasn't pregnant. She didn't know and advised me to see my doctor.

As I crawled in the car and told Phil the news we were both puzzled. What were we supposed to think now? I was slightly hopeful. We drove to the doctor's office in silence, each of us inwardly theorizing about what this all meant and what the doctor might tell us.

"How are you feeling today?" Lynne inquired. One quick glance had already revealed the answer. My face was ashen white and my nose was running. To sum it up, I looked absolutely awful.

"Well, I still feel pretty queasy and this cold doesn't help." I reported the results of the pregnancy test done at the clinic that morning. I could tell she was pleasantly surprised. Once again my exam showed everything looked normal. By all appearances I was still pregnant. I breathed a sigh of relief.

"Now we need to see what's going on inside, so we'll schedule another sonogram for you." My heart sank. My last visit in that room was still indelibly etched in my memory. I was given the huge glass again and instructed to drink at least three of them filled with water. These large amounts of water pushed the internal organs out of the way so the technician could see the uterus better.

This time I had the good sense to use tap water. I didn't get so cold. Phil and I waited nervously for them to call us. I couldn't bear to pick up the baby magazines. I leafed through old issues of Time hoping I'd calm down. Phil glanced at me urging me to drink more.

"Sue, you can come back now," the nurse instructed as she peeked through the door. After a few minutes, Jessie met us in the room and she began the process all over. This time, Phil raised many questions about what we were seeing. We were able to understand better what the screen displayed. Soon Lynne joined us and chimed in with explanations.

My uterus was no longer filled with blood. In fact, the appearance of everything had drastically changed. The sac we saw on November seventeenth was gone but now there was a small dark ball at the entrance of my right fallopian tube. I tentatively asked, "Is that...?"

"Well, it could be a baby," Lynne interrupted, reading my thoughts, "or it could be a blood clot. If it's a baby, this might be a tubal pregnancy. I can't tell whether it's in utero or not." Jessie tried to get a better picture but the one we were seeing continued to present us with more questions and doubts. I was told to change and come back to Lynne's office.

Lynne's sober look preempted her words. Phil and I knew the news wasn't good. Lynne sighed. "What can I say? We still really don't know what's happening. We're not sure if that's a baby we saw on the screen or not. It could be a blood clot for all we know. If it is a baby, you might have a tubal pregnancy."

"What does that mean?" I interjected.

"The baby may not be inside the uterine wall. If it

grows one way, into your tubes, it could be dangerous for you, cause you pain and require surgery. If it grows the other way, you just might be all right. We just don't know for sure, so we'll have to wait a few days. If it is a baby, it will have grown enough by then that we'll be able to tell. In the meantime, if you have any sharp pain in your stomach at all, call us immediately."

Phil asked a few more questions as I sat numbly listening in disappointment. Lynne realized she was not able to give a lot of conclusive answers and honestly admitted this. "Sue, I know I'm not giving you much to go on. All I can say is, only God knows what is happening."

I nodded in tearful agreement and we went back to the appointment desk to set up a time for another sonogram. Phil took care of everything as I slowly walked back to the car.

On the way home we reviewed all that we were told, trying to get it firmly in our minds so we could explain it intelligently to other people. This was a practice we had adopted after each visit to the clinic. It helped us understand and digest all the varied information we had received that day. The conversation also speeded our acceptance of the news.

We decided we would try and present only the basic facts since the prognosis was so nebulous. The phone calls slowed somewhat. People were beginning to realize that it was taxing to make explanations over and over.

Weakness, both emotional and physical, plagued me. I was continually on the verge of tears and avoided intense conversations or explanations. I tried to put up a brave front. If I showed my true feelings, I reasoned, the congregation would only be depressed and burdened. Phil gave a brief prayer request concerning my condition in his morning sermon. He tried to be upbeat, but people sensed the lurking dangers and doubts surrounding his optimistic reports. Inwardly, my soul cried. It was the beginning of what was to be one long, muffled cry.

Normality was slowly fading from my life. Everything seemed to be in turmoil from my perspective. Our three children were sensing this. They wanted to know whether or not I had lost the baby. How do you explain all these unanswerable things to a seven and nine-year-old? Our 14 month-old Jonathan couldn't verbally ask questions, but he too seemed to know that something was wrong. As time went on he began clinging to me more and more. His large blue eyes reflected questions when he would see me sitting on the couch crying. As tears flowed, he would try to comfort me by his closeness, laying his head tenderly on my lap.

New emotions and thoughts came to me constantly. I continued my daily Bible reading, but the usual comfort wasn't there. I couldn't seem to find what I needed. "What's wrong with me? If I can't find what I need for comfort here in God's Word then I'm really in a bad situation. I should be able to get comfort! Am I reading in the wrong places? Am I shutting off God?" Fear began to build, then guilt over having such thoughts. And after the guilt depressing numbness. Confusion plagued me. Anxiously I replayed the doctor's visits in my mind. "How could this be? Was I pregnant or not? I couldn't believe there was an inbetween. I felt I was in limbo. Isn't this just a bad nightmare? Why can't I shake these thoughts?"

I remember one woman coming over to encourage me. I tried not to show how blue I was but it was getting more difficult to hide my feelings. As our visit was ending, she smiled, walked through the doorway and said, "You know, Sue, God must really love you. He knows you're special and has allowed this in love because of that." Cynically I thought, "Well, I don't feel special," and said goodbye.

The following morning, dawn brought no relief. I slipped out of bed leaving Phil asleep. With a heaviness still blanketing my thoughts I struggled to find comfort to ease my troubled mind. With resolve I settled in my favorite spot and prayed. "Oh dear Father. I feel so discouraged. I don't know what I'm asking for You to do but I know that something in my heart will have to change soon. I have tried finding comfort in the things people say but it just isn't there. Father, You alone know my heart. You know how sad and confused I am. I am frustrated and impatient. I want all the answers now to my situation, in black and white. Please, Lord, as I open Your Word right now, speak to me. Show me what You want me to think and feel. Please open my heart and help me as only You can do."

Slowly, I flipped open my Bible to the book of Psalms. It was like an old friend during difficult times. In chapter twenty, the fourth verse practically jumped from the page and into my heart. "May He give you the desire of your heart and make all your plans succeed."

"Yes, Lord, you know what plans we have."

I paused and meditated on that verse, particularly the word "plans." God was answering my prayer. As I searched the scriptures, God began to remind me of plans that were ordained by Him and those that weren't. Peace crept in as I read. I sensed that God was showing me something important, so I grabbed my notebook and wrote down these thoughts concerning the following verses:

PLANS

Exodus 26:30: the tabernacle was set up according to a specific plan.

Job 42:2: Job knew God had plans and that God's plans can never be thwarted.

Psalm 64:6: even the wicked have plans (which they think are perfect).

Psalm 140:4: wicked men make plans to trip up the righteous.

Proverbs 14:22: the plans of the wicked will fail, but those who plan good will find love and faithfulness.

Proverbs 21:30: there is no wisdom or plan that can succeed against the Lord.

Jeremiah 18:11,12: the Lord devises plans to punish those who disobey Him while they stubbornly continue in their own way.

Psalm 33:11: God's plans stand firm forever.

Proverbs 16:9: we can plan, but the Lord truly determines our steps.

Isaiah 29:15: we can't hide our plans from God.

Isaiah 30:1: we will have woe if we carry out plans that aren't God's.

Jeremiah 29:11: God knows the plan He has for us.

At the top of the page I wrote Proverbs 16:3: "Commit to the Lord whatever you do and your plans will succeed," and I also quoted Psalm 20:4: "May He give you the desire of your heart and make all your plans succeed."

What joy flooded me when I finished my reading! God knew just what I needed. I hadn't been at peace before because I was beginning to think that God had abandoned me or that He didn't really know what my desires were. Just as Satan tempted Eve with doubt, I had also listened. But God broke down Satan's arguments one by one. I was assured that God knew and cared about what was going on inside me, both physically and emotionally. Trusting and waiting was the best I could do.

As the peace of God continued to course through me, I decided to call my Mom and share with her what I had found in my reading. Mom and I were so close. We were more like best friends than mother and daughter. I knew she sensed my turmoil so I was sure my call would cheer her. Excitedly I shared all that God had shown me. Joyful tears included relief, knowing that anyone could heal and take care of her daughter's body, but only God could comfort her heart. She shared in my quiet victory and we were both encouraged. With the click of the receiver my thoughts turned to Phil. I walked back to the bedroom to wake him and report the morning's victory.

In my daily journal I entered, "So the only thing I'm sure of at this point is my trust in God. This is a time of learning to lean on Him and wait for His timing. My human side would say 'I want to know now,' but the Holy Spirit quietly whispers 'wait and trust.'"

4
Temporary Twins

November 23 when I called the office to re-check the appointed time for my ultrasound they informed me that the equipment was malfunctioning. My heart sank. I was hoping to get some answers about my condition today. The receptionist continued. "Lynne has made other arrangements. She wants you to go across the street to the hospital and have it done." I was relieved.

I had now developed a technique in my water drinking routine. I chose my favorite large glass, filled it with tap water and drank two glasses before we left the house. Once we arrived at the hospital, I drank another glass. By now, I had learned I didn't have to drink as much as they said or drink it so far in advance. Finishing my last sip, I prayed they would call my name soon. I tried to divert my thoughts by working on a cross stitch design.

Lynne meandered into the beige waiting room with her typical grin beaming from a suntanned face. Her enormous blue eyes seemed permanently frozen in a wide-open startled position. When she spoke her blond eyebrows synchronized with her moving hands. She had certainly lifted our spirits many times by her off-beat sense of humor and casual manner. "Drinking again, huh, Sue?" she joked.

"No, don't you know pastors' wives aren't allowed?" I quipped, This jesting was an unspoken procedure for us both and seemed to ease the tension. Obviously my case had been on her mind and puzzled her. Maybe she felt slightly guilty for not having all the answers. As usual I was comforted by her presence and she explained that Phil wouldn't be allowed into the room because of hospital policy. With resignation and some resentment he sat down. At least he came prepared. After our long waits at the doctor's office he decided to utilize his time. As I walked from the room my backward glance revealed Phil busily carving a wooden plaque.

I lay down on an elevated hospital bed. "At least this room's not so cold," I sighed. The ultrasound technician flipped on the instruments and began her work. The combined waiting and nervousness made it very hard to lie still. I tried to squelch the urge to jump off the table and run to the bathroom. Lynne and I expectantly turned our faces to the screen. I'm sure she was just as curious as I at what this sonogram would reveal.

The picture looked so strange. The technician explained to Lynne and me that their equipment showed the blacks and whites in reverse. What showed up black on the equipment in the doctor's office came out white on this screen. We searched for the precious thing we all yearned to see, a sac with a baby. My heart flip-flopped when I spied a tiny pulsing dot. Lynne confirmed what my eyes saw. "There's the baby! I really am pregnant," I thought. It was like hearing I was pregnant for the first time.

Lynne explained to the technician the unique features surrounding my case.

"How can this be?" I questioned. "I thought there was no baby. We couldn't see a sac the other day. How did this baby show up?"

"You know what I think, Sue?" Lynne proclaimed with animation. "I'm beginning to believe that you had twins, lost one, and this is the remaining baby!"

"You're kidding! Do you think that's where all the bleeding has been coming from?"

"I think so," she surmised. As the technician left the room I grabbed Lynne and hugged her.

"I'm so happy! You know, Lynne, I've done an awful lot of praying and just the other day God reminded me that He was sovereign and He would do whatever He wished. I was at peace with whatever He would give us. Today He answered my heart's desire! May I go to the bathroom now?"

"Yes!" Lynne laughed as I sped past her.

In the waiting room Lynne was excitedly explaining to a beaming Phil what we saw on the screen. "I got to thinking about you the other day, Sue, as I was reading through some case histories. One woman had twins, lost one and kept the other. I guessed this might be happening to you."

Phil's face revealed the same happy disbelief I had felt. Overjoyed, our happy trio boarded the hospital elevator.

The trip home from the hospital was filled with reflections, laughing, unashamed singing and shouting of God's victory. Bright sunlight flooded through our open windows, putting an invisible spotlight on our duet. Cars whisked by, oblivious to our exuberance. What a miracle! None of this would have been possible if I had gone ahead with the D and C the doctor had recommended. We were awed at the wisdom God gave me that day in the doctor's office and thanked Him robustly for His direction. Yes, He knew our plans and His, and he could be trusted to bring them to pass in spite of all circumstances. Yes, He is a God that can be trusted.

Turning the corner to our street, we broke out in praise with my favorite hymn, "Count Your Blessings." We turned to each other and beheld our two slobbery, tear-stained faces. Laughing, we sealed our joy with a kiss and headed home to spread the news of our exhilarating miracle to everyone.

Now I could dig into my maternity clothes and proudly wear them.

5
New Hope

There were still lingering doubts disturbing me. I was bleeding again. I hoped it would subside, but the nagging spotting continued. The roller coaster of emotions surged up and down. Sometimes I just wanted to get off.

I discussed my jogging again with Lynne and she still assured me it wouldn't hurt the baby. She did suggest that I stop for three to four weeks, mentioning that during this time the baby was implanting itself in the uterus and the extra jarring might possibly hinder this process. Physical exercise had become such a daily habit, I found it impossible to give up every acitivity, so bicycling and brisk walking became my safe alternatives.

People pleasingly commented on the bulge that was beginning to show. It was nice to see that physically I looked like a woman with child.

The spotting slowed, but continued. It never followed a certain pattern. Physical activity sometimes prompted more bleeding, yet other times it would happen if I was just sitting still.

Many people in the church didn't know all the details about my pregnancy. It seemed easier than having to explain all the difficulties. We usually gave progress reports in our Wednesday evening prayer services, but even those people had no idea of the turmoil Phil and I had been through.

In spite of the positive signs, I continued to hold a reserve on my feelings concerning the probability of carrying the baby to term. This pregnancy was just so different. It was very unsettling.

Phil and I had a practice of going to the church foyer after his messages and greeting departing people together. I enjoyed this because it presented us as we truly were, unified in this ministry God had given us. Now, it was increasingly difficult to answer the typical questions.

One Sunday, Phil had given a brief update on my condition and after his message we walked to the foyer and took our places. As I shook hands and exchanged greetings with people, a young woman in a maternity outfit appeared. She seemed oblivious to the serious undertones of my condition. "When are you due?" she asked. Of course this question is asked repeatedly throughout every pregnancy, but this time it was different. It almost seemed like a slap in the face.

Flustered, I stammered, "Well, if the baby makes it that long, it'll be born in July." She gleefully related that she was due just a few weeks after that. Suddenly, I was fully aware of my own doubts.

God was weaving so many things into my character. The peace of God still lingered. No matter how my feelings varied, I still rested in His sovereignty and clung to it tenaciously.

Phil was apprehensively allowing himself to become more attached to this little miracle baby too. We wondered what this child would be like and what plans God would have for him. Certainly, any kid who could survive this ordeal would be special. We reminisced about my previous pregnancy when I carried Jonathan and commented on how very different his was. One night, as we lay in bed discussing the day's activities and our future dreams, Phil asked, "I wonder

39

what this baby will be like. Do you think his temperament will be similar to the other children?"

Jokingly, I responded, "No. After all the trouble we've already gone through with this one, we'll probably get into the labor room, I'll deliver and it'll be the crankiest kid you ever met!" We laughed hysterically.

Holly came home from school one day and questioned, "Mommy, my teacher wants to know what in the world is going on. One day at prayer request time I tell her you're pregnant. The next day, I tell her you lost the baby. Now, I tell her that you had twins. She wants to know just what is true!" Chuckling, I tried to explain the whole situation to her. I assured her it was just as confusing to me at times, but all we could do was take it one day at a time. My explanation seemed to only slightly relieve her confusion.

My December 15th doctor's visit began uneventfully. Although the spotting continued, the exam showed it wasn't fresh blood, therefore the baby wasn't being harmed. The scales showed I had gained four pounds! It was one of those few times in life I didn't mind gaining weight. Nausea was still twisting my stomach but seemed to be lessening in its intensity.

A little tension was added when Ann, the other midwife, wanted to check for a heartbeat. My heart pounded like the base line in a heavy metal song. Was it too early? What would I do if we heard nothing? What if I was carrying a dead baby?

Ann rubbed the dopler (microphone) over my abdomen. We all waited in tense silence. "Oh Lord, please let me hear the heartbeat," I prayed. I searched Ann's brown eyes for encouragement. There was none to be found. She pushed and moved the dopler from one side to another, pressing harder each time. I heard all the noises from my intestines digesting my last meal, yet no heartbeat. She was almost ready to quit when a rapid thumping was distinctly heard. Phil, Ann and I breathed a sigh of relief.

At that moment, our hope blossomed. I allowed myself the luxury of it. "Yes siree, there's a real live baby in there." I giggled as I patted my tummy.

Soon after the visit, I rearranged my closet. Behind closed doors I acted out my own steps of faith. One by one I folded up my size sevens and nines and plunged into the maternity clothes. Carefully I hung each article up and when all was done, prayed I would have need for them. I acknowledged that day that this pregnancy was going to continue, though I didn't know for how long.

Each passing day brought new confidence. Spotting was accepted as commonplace to me now and alarm over it faded. My waiting period for jogging was over and I joyfully started again.

6
Christmas Blues

Ordinarily Christmas was my favorite time of year and I relished every day of the season. As soon as Thanksgiving had passed, I would anticipate every day until December first when traditionally all the Christmas decorations would come out. By three or four p.m. of the same day the house would be resplendent with Christmas trimming including the tree. Many nights I would stay up after all was quiet and gaze at the beautiful blue lights on the tree. The calming glow they emitted would mesmerize me and I would reminisce of past Christmases and happy memories.

This year was different. It was almost a chore to go through all the traditional duties. I was still feeling queasy, dulling my desire to cook the family Christmas favorites. All my thoughts centered around the baby and the uncertainties of the situation.

A few evenings I stayed up, played the Christmas music albums and tried to drum up feelings of the Christmas spirit. It didn't work. Even my tree-watching vigil changed. Instead of reminiscing of happy Christmases in the past, unsettling doubts of the future crept in. "Would this child ever live to celebrate a Christmas with us?" Over and over I pushed those thoughts from my mind and dismissed the pessimism they prompted. I wanted to be joyous and happy but each glance in the mirror brought only doubts. I just couldn't feel secure about this child.

Traditionally, Christmas was filled with family gatherings. Our church choir busily worked on a cantata. Church fellowships were frequent and sharing in intimate conversations was always refreshing. It was a busy time of year.

Phil's niece, Mandy, arrived for her annual visit. A few day later, his sister, Judell, flew in from California to spend a week as she did every year. One of our family traditions included a two hour trip to Disney World near Orlando. This had started when Mandy was very young and even though she was now a teenager we never tired of this annual Disney pilgrimage. We counted the days and soon December 19th, Disney Day, was here.

We decided to visit Epcot Center, the newest portion of Disney World. Phil and I always enjoyed these trips to Disney. It was our one totally frivolous day out of the year. The fear we both silently harbored was that my condition would keep us from making the trip. Lynne had assured us during my last visit that it would be safe to go. We resolved to get a wheelchair if I grew too tired.

At six a.m. on December 19th, we met at Phil's parents' house and decided who would ride in the two cars. Judell opted to ride with Jonathan, Phil and me. Holly and David gleefully jumped into the other car with Phil's parents, his brother Tim and his niece Mandy.

It was relaxing for me to have a break from all serious considerations about my pregnancy. We also looked forward to the traditional breakfast along the way. We pulled into a fast food restaurant in Tampa. Jokes about previous visits to Disney World and visions of what Epcot would be like dominated our conversation. We had heard how crowded it was, especially during the holiday season, but hoped we'd miss the larger crowds by going before Christmas Day. With amply filled stomachs and growing excitement we piled back into our two cars and headed for Epcot.

Judell knew of the difficulties I'd been having. She wondered whether our jog two days earlier was wise. I assured her of Lynne's okay and mentioned that some women told me they spotted during their entire pregnancy. "Is riding in the car okay?" she asked.

"Sure," I answered firmly. "We asked Lynne. She gave her stamp of approval."

Tampa was now behind us and we were just outside the city limits. Phil and Judell were engaged in a heavy conversation about family matters. I was listening intently when I felt another rushing sensation. Without speaking, I shifted position, thinking it would quickly pass.

"Boy," I thought, "I sure am hyper about this. You're okay, Sue. Settle down." But soon, I realized that this was not the typical spotting I'd been having.

"Phil, I'm bleeding a little heavier than usual," I stated tensely. "Could you pull over at the next gas station just so I can check to make sure?" I didn't want to alarm him unduly.

"Maybe I'd be okay," I thought.

"Are you sure we need to?" he asked, glancing at his watch. "Can't you wait until we get there? Isn't it like what you've been having all along?"

Solemnly I replied, "No, honey. This is different. It's heavier than usual." I must have sounded too casual.

He glanced at my tensed face and knew it was serious. We put on the turn signal at the next exit so Phil's parents would follow.

The restrooms were located at the right side of the gas station. Swiftly we pulled into the adjacent parking lot. When my foot touched the pavement, my heart flip-flopped. It was gravely apparent my bleeding was heavy. The sensation reminded me of the feeling I had when my water broke. I quickly ran to the bathroom.

The room was dirty and dimly lit. Scattered papers made a messy carpet. Dripping water continued painting a deeper brown hue in the rust-stained porcelain sink. Grit and grime were everywhere, mingling perfectly with the foul odor and graffiti on the walls. I shut the finger-printed door and clicked on the light with no results. Fumbling in the darkness for the doorknob, I yelled out to Phil, "The light doesn't work! Come and stand by the door and hold it ajar so I can see. Don't let anyone come in."

Another surge came. "Oh Lord! What should I do?" This bleeding was so heavy. I reached for toilet paper and grasped at empty air. "Oh no. Now what do I do?" The situation closed in on me. Tears once again dripped from my face and mingled with the grime on the green floor as I sobbed uncontrollably.

By this time, Phil's mother came in to check on me. She was a Licensed Practical Nurse and I was often comforted by her medical knowledge. As she stepped into my hastily made emergency room I cried, "Oh Mom! I must be losing the baby! The bleeding won't quit! What should I do? There's not even any toilet paper!" Her eyes fastened on me with a look of desperate concern. She normally didn't fluster easily. I knew it must be serious.

"I'll see if I can get you some paper towels." She turned and ran. I look at Phil silhouetted in the doorway.

"What should we do? Maybe this will stop." I added hopefully, "I don't want to lose the baby and I don't want to turn around and go all the way back home." Varying emotions crowded in at once in a confusing pattern. Everything was jumbled.

"Sue!" Phil cried wth a whine of frustation. "We

can't possibly go to Epcot now. We need to get you home and to the doctor." He stepped into the filthy room and placed his hand on my shoulder.

"Oh Honey!" I cried in disappointment. "Why did this have to happen today? And why this crummy bathroom? If I am going to lose the baby, why couldn't it at least have happened at home and at another time?"

Phil moved closer and placed his strong arms around my shoulders resting his head on mine. My tears flowed as he shared in my sorrow. "I know how you feel, Hon. I know how much you looked forward to going to Epcot, but we just can't go. What if we got there and you started hemorrhaging?" His tone softened with tenderness. "Besides, you wouldn't enjoy it. You'd be wondering what happened and you'd also be exhausted from all this emotional and physical strain. I'll tell Mom and Dad to go on with the kids and Judell. We'll take Jonathan and go home and call the doctor's office."

I agreed tearfully. My own disappointment was mixed with fear for the baby. I felt like a kid waking up from a nightmare. Only this was real and I couldn't close my eyes to erase the situation. I was angry that our special tradition was ruined. I wanted to kick something or blame someone. Maybe I'd feel better.

Phil's mother soon returned with paper towels and helped me get back into the car. Looks of concern filled everyone's faces as I peered through tear-stained eyes and waved goodbye to the family. Epcot would have three less people.

Phil put my car seat into a reclining position and I tried to elevate my feet. All I could do was cry. For several long minutes we said nothing. Phil squeezed my hand tightly. Worry etched lines in his forehead. Jonathan cried a little and finally settled down, staring up at me quietly.

"Honey, I'm just so disappointed! I have such mixed emotions. I know I should be more concerned about the baby, but I'm more disappointed about missing Epcot than anything else right now. I was looking forward to this day so much."

"I know, Honey. I was too. Maybe the bleeding will stop and we can make the trip later in the day. We'll see what the doctor says." Phil was being unrealistically hopeful. The disappointment had made both of us childish enough to throw reason out the window.

"It just won't seem like Christmas to me now," I said. "It's not just the trip I'm missing. It's the tradition. I wanted to be there to share in our tradition." Somehow, I knew there was no reasonable hope we could come all the way back even if the bleeding did stop.

Phil sympathetically agreed. We shared together in disappointment and tears. Optimistically we thought this might not mean the loss of the baby but the dark fears were hard to block out. As we drove home we agonized together over our confused emotion. The more time passed, the more our disapointment over the spoiled outing was swallowed up by concern for the baby.

Our brown Honda slowed. The car in front of us came closer as we drove at a turtle's pace. "Oh no!" Phil irritatedly sighed, "a traffic jam! There must be an accident ahead."

Jonathan awoke as the sun baked our car several degrees hotter. My head felt like a windowpane. Jonathan's crying was the hammer ready to smash it. Another surge of blood came. I shifted my feet higher up on the dash.

"Oh great!" I added. "That's all we need! What if I start to lose the baby here in the middle of this traffic jam! I felt panicky. We couldn't do a thing. I prayed it would clear soon. I slid my feet higher on the dash hoping it would slow the bleeding. Beads of sweat trickled down our faces. Inch by inch we edged slowly ahead and soon progressed past the stalled vehicle. As the wind rushed in and the car hummed its fifty mile an hour tune, Jonathan was lulled back into sleep.

Once at home, I gathered myself like an eggshell and walked hunched over·to the house. Phil quickly unlocked the door and put Jonathan in bed. We phoned Lynne at the doctor's office.

"Come to the office right away," she instructed with urgency. We managed to get a friend to watch Jonathan.

We drove the now familiar route to the clinic in a continued state of emotional numbness. I stepped out of our parked car. Each slow step to the office door brought more tension. Were my shoes filled with cement?

I told Lynne all that had transpired. Her blonde curls bounced as she nodded, recording all the information on my ever-thickening chart. "Lay back and let's see if we can hear a heartbeat."

The three of us strained to hear that precious "thump, thump, thump." Seconds passed, minutes. As the dopler passed the lower portion of my abdomen we tensed, and then "thump, thump, thump."

"Whew!"

We sighed in tension-breaking unison. Each upturned eyebrow relaxed. "Thank You, Lord!" I thought. "At least I still have the baby!"

Lynne examined me again and noted my cervix was still tight and closed, a good sign. She wasn't going to speculate about my condition yet. If she was encouraged, her face didn't show it. "Let's get another sonogram, Sue, and see what's happening now."

The familiar blue glass was handed to me again as Lynne leaked a controlled smile. Each tiny swallow felt like a gallon. I'd become adept at drinking the water in minutes. I sloshed back to the darkened ultrasound room and the familiar white-sheeted bed. Again we viewed the fuzzy black and white screen with apprehension. Lynne called in a doctor and they silently watched. I didn't like their furtive glances and whispers. We definitely saw the baby. His (or her) little heart could be seen thumping away like a pump pushing water through a valve. Its steadiness encouraged me. A dark balloon-like shape came into view. It seemed deflated. By now I knew that was an empty sac. A pang of sadness swelled within me.

"That was a baby's vacant home." I shifted my position. The bed always made my back ache. As I turned, I spied something else on the screen. "Hey," I thought to myself, "is that another sac in there?" I strained to see more.

Abruptly Lynne spoke, leaving my question unanswered. "You can change now, Sue. You and Phil come to my office and we'll talk."

"Now what is going on?" I wondered. "Why didn't she just give a straight answer? What's the big mystery?" I pulled my blue-flowered maternity blouse over my head. Phil's narrowed eyes signaled he was having the same thoughts.

As we entered Lynne's room, I searched for a bit of encouragement on her face. There was none.

"Well," Lynne started, "you're not going to believe this, but today we saw another sac." She shook her head in disbelief. Her hands flew up in an exasperated fashion. "We think you've had triplets and lost two."

Were my ears betraying me? I thought this couldn't be possible! I was too shocked to reply. My ashen face turned to Phil. Sensing my speechlessness, he collected his thoughts and spoke. One rapid fire question came after another.

"Why hadn't they seen this before? Does this mean the present baby is okay? When these other sacs ripped, did it injure the baby? Has this ever happened before?"

"Lynne tried her best to answer his questions. She explained that the bleeding was from one of those sacs, which of them they didn't know.

"Oh good," I sighed, "then the baby will be all right."

Lynne's words jolted me out of my optimistic pipe dream. "Sue, we're going to have to watch you very closely from now on. We'll have to check with blood tests to make certain you're not losing too much blood. We also want to make sure you are clotting properly. You'll need to come in once a week from now on." This wasn't exactly the hopeful information I was looking for. I was excited that I still had the baby after all of this, but it was obvious Lynne saw no reason for jubilation. The situation was still very serious and she wanted us to know that.

My optimism was dying. The urge to cry seized me. Tears stole from the corners of my eyes. I resentfully brushed them away. How I wished I could control myself better.

"How are you feeling emotionally about all this, Sue?" Lynne paused. "I know you're a pastor's wife and you feel you need to be smiling all the time. We all have our limits, Sue. Just because of your position in the church you don't always have to have it all together. It's okay to cry. You don't have to tell your congregation everything. There are some things you can keep private. What do you think?"

"Well, I think I just hit my limit," I admitted honestly. I avoided looking into her searching eyes. "The hardest part for me is going to the foyer, shaking hands and trying to answer people's questions. It's so hard to keep the lid on my emotions. Sometimes I just want to go and hide. I'm tired of answering questions!" Phil agreed and I sighed with relief. I felt like a cement truck full of responsibility had parked somewhere beside my shoulders.

"You need to go home, stay in bed for a few days and get some rest. We'll see you in a week." She laid a hand on my shoudler. "Are you sure you don't have any other questions?" I struggled to regain sensibility.

"Oh yeah," I remembered, "we always go over to my parents' place to celebrate Christmas day. Is that all right? They live in Lake Wales."

"How far away is that? How long does it usually take you to get there?"

"Usually about two hours." Phil commented in forced optimism. "Don't worry, I'll make sure she's good." He patted my arm and gave me a wink.

Lynne squinched in a half frown. "I'll leave that decision to you. I'd rather you didn't but if it's that important to you I'll say okay, only on one condition. You need to stay in bed the next few days. If your bleeding subsides, then you can leave. If it doesn't, I'm afraid you'll have to stay home. Will you be sure and not do anything strenuous?" She shuffled through some white papers from my file. "Your blood count is down and so is your energy level, so you need to lie around."

"I'll make certain she rests," Phil assured as he glanced at me. Handing me another kleenex to wipe my swollen eyes, Lynne got up from her seat. She stepped over to us and assisted Phil in helping me get up. Patting my back, Lynne added, "Hey, take it easy. Remember, only God knows."

"Yeah," I mumbled. "Only God knows" was becoming our favorite parting phrase.

"And, uh, Merry Christmas," Lynne offhandedly wished. I gave her arm a squeeze. I knew she cared. In her own way she tried to make me feel better. I sensed her frustation over it all.

The route home was once again visited by our little car bearing its weary occupants. Christmas reds and greens cheered every view in gaudy decoration, but the season had lost its color for me. I felt color blind and what's more, I didn't care. I wanted Christmas to be over. Reluctantly we returned home. I stepped on the stone doorstep and opened the brown door. My eyes rested on the Christmas tree. How bewildered it looked with its twinkling blue lights off. Even the pine smell had faded. The day was overcast and that cloud lingered inside our home. I wanted to forget it was Christmas. I sought escape from it all as I slumped wearily onto the bed.

Debbie, our church secretary and "adopted" daughter knocked at the front door. I knew she was bringing Jonathan home but I avoided an appearance. I wasn't sure I could handle seeing her pixie smile fade into tears. Muffled sounds of Phil explaining the latest doctor's report seeped through the crack underneath our bedroom door.

"Sue," Debbie hesitatingly asked, "I know you're tired, but can I just come in and give you a hug?" I wiped the tears hastily from my eyes.

"Yes, come on in." Debbie's youthful round face was devoid of its normal welcoming twinkles. Tears glistened from the corners of her green eyes. I buried my head in her thick brown hair as our tears mingled.

"I'm sorry, Sue. Phil told me what happened. Are you doing okay?"

"Yeah, I...I guess I'll be all right. I'm so disappointed, Deb. I feel like every ounce of energy has been drained from me. I mean, can you believe it? Me with triplets? This whole thing is just so unreal!" She heaved a sigh as another tear drizzled down her cheek.

"Oh Sue, I'm praying for you. I wish there was more I could do. Please, please let me know if I can help in any other ways. I'll watch the kids, cook, clean, anything. You name it."

"I know, Deb. You're so sweet, Believe me, I'm feeling so weak I don't think I'll be able to do much so I'll give you a call when I need you."

She gave me a final hug then turned and left. Phil entered, his expressions blanketed with weariness. "I put Jonathan to bed," he informed. "Poor little guy was awfully tired. I think he slept the whole time we were at the doctor's office. Debbie said he was no trouble."

"I suppose we should try and get some rest," I added.

"Yeah, I guess so," Phil answered, staring at the floor. He slumped into bed.

I again sought refuge in his arms as the emotions of the day swept over me. Using his chest for my pillow, I lay still, too tired to utter a word. We lay there, snuggled under our brown satin comforter with only the unison sound of our breathing audible in the room. Phil's sighs turned into gentle, steady breathing. Sleep had overtaken him. Release wasn't as easy for me. The quiet bed yielded no peace. Those brown sheets reflected my mood. Everything looked dull, colorless, brown to me. My throbbing head prevented sleep.

"I might as well get up and go out so Phil can at least get some rest," I concluded. As I rose, a lightheadedness left me spinning. Cautiously I moved, closed the door behind me and made my way to the living room couch. There they were again, all the reminders that Christmas was still here. The decorations seemed to grin cynically. The warmth of the garland was gone. The rich reds, greens and golds looked gaudy, out of place. That tree rudely stood in front of me, straight and tall. Obnoxiously it shouted,

"Merry Christmas."

"How could this holiday possibly be merry?" I quizzed myself. The whole season seemed an intrusion to me and I selfishly wished it was over. "How can I celebrate a birth when I may be awaiting a death?" Penetrating questions continued to flow through my mind. I had to remind myself of God's perspective on this whole situation or I would depress everyone around me. "Just what is Christmas anyway, Sue," I asked. "When everything precious, or special, or traditional is taken away, isn't Christmas still here?" My conscience waged a war. Fear answered. "But what if I lose the baby? How can I be happy? I'm so afraid I'm going to lose the baby on Christmas Day!"

The Holy Spirit seemed to whisper, "And who else lost a beloved child? Don't you think your Heavenly Father can truly empathize with you? Don't you think Mary knew what a mixed blessing it was to give birth to a child that was born to die? Don't you think others have felt the fears and doubts that you feel?"

My fears took flight again. Phil stepped into the dimly lit room. "You didn't sleep very long, Hon," I noted, surveying the dark circles under his eyes.

"I couldn't," he replied. "I kept hoping this was all a nightmare and that when I woke up, everything would be fine. Then I awakened and realized where I was and what had happened." He paused, slumped next to me on the couch. "I wonder if they're having fun at Epcot."

Our minds raced back into memories of previous visits. The vivid colors, multicolored flowers, flashes of Mickey's face, enticing aromas of food, mounting excitement from a new ride, even the long lines seemed appealing. This kaleidoscope of memories pained us because this year we weren't participants. I brushed the thoughts aside and tried to encourage Phil by relating my previous conversation with myself. His saddened expression changed. Lines faded. He joined in my upward outlook.

I slipped off the couch, leaned over and plugged in the twinkling blue lights. The room welcomed the cheerful glow. Light danced around the ornaments. They came alive with sparkles of color. I nestled back into Phil's open arms and our spirits revived as our thoughts wandered back to that first Christmas long ago when Jesus was born. We had so much to be happy about. Did bad circumstances kill their joy about His birth?

"Hey," I interrupted, "why don't you start a fire and we'll sing Christmas carols?"

"That's a good idea," Phil agreed and soon he had a crackling fire going in our wood stove. Tension and fear melted away as we sat, hypnotized by the orange glow. The blue hue of the tree lights mingled with the firelight.

Our living room danced with warmth. Once again, it looked inviting to me. The slate stone hearth and wall reflected the colors back. Five handmade stockings hung from the stones behind the wood stove, their cheery colors highlighted by the fire's reflection. Red poinsettias peeked out from rich evergreen hung around the chair-rail panelling.

"Silent Night," "Away In A Manger" and "Joy To The World" filled the room. Our alto and tenor voices blended together in praise with tears intertwining the notes. God had intervened. He put a "new song" in our hearts, reaching our inner core. The restlessness and grief were stilled. Our oneness seemed even more solid by focusing on the true meaning of Christmas, Christ Himself. After all, wasn't Jesus stripped of everything when He humbled Himself and came in human form as that tiny, innocent baby? Christmas doesn't merely consist of twinkling lights, varied colors, Christmas carols and gifts. It's Jesus and all that His coming means.

In that moment, previous concepts of Christmas gave way to deeper, more mature thoughts. I guess I gave up all my little childish toys. I couldn't just look forward to opening gifts. Who was the reason we had gifts? Jesus. He is all that matters. Though we faced our baby's possible death in this year, we could carry on in spite of it all. Christ's birth, death, and final resurrection gave unalterable hope that we would see our babies in heaven.

A knock on the door interrupted our thoughts. Phil answered. "Hi, Philsky," a cheerful voice greeted. In bounced our friend Johnnie.

"Nancy and I thought you guys might like this food," he said as he handed over several dishes. Delicious aromas drifted through the room.

"Mmmm. Johnnie, it smells great. That was really sweet of you guys. Please tell Nancy how much we appreciate it...especially today," I added, hoping he'd ask more.

"Sue, you look terrible! Are you all right?" There was no way I could fool anyone today.

As I rehashed the whole day's incidents, Johnnie's impish smile faded. His green eyes narrowed with deep concern. He never was good at hiding his big heart. "Gee, Sue, that's terrible. We'll sure pray everything turns out okay." As we walked toward the door, he turned and quipped, "Hey. Take care of yourself. Don't go and croak on us. It'd spoil Christmas!" He jaunted out the door and into his car. Knowing Johnnie, he went home in tears.

7
Fear, The Unwelcome Advisor

December 24th we made our final Christmas preparations, wrapping gifts and delivering presents. We had a tightly packed schedule of annual Christmas celebrations. The candlelight Christmas Eve church service headed the agenda. After church, we gathered at the home of Phil's parents with the relatives and opened our gifts from them. The following morning, we awakened the kids early, had Christmas with our own family and then headed to Lake Wales to spend the day with my family. On our way we always stopped midway and had breakfast at a restaurant.

This year, I dreaded it all. I kept fighting back the fear that I would lose the baby on Christmas Day. Dread overwhelmed me every time I thought about passing that certain gas station beyond Tampa where I started bleeding six days before. I chided myself for thinking so superstitiously about crossing that same pathway again. "Of course I would not start bleeding again. That was just a rare incident and wouldn't repeat itself," I thought. But logic wasn't winning too much these days. It was my heart and emotions that strongly controlled me. "Get yourself together, Sue," I instructed. "Once you get dressed up and ready to go you'll feel better." Time was slipping away. I needed to get ready for the service and quit daydreaming.

I examined my wardrobe. Again I asked, "Should I wear maternity clothes or not? I could still fit into some of my looser things. I chose a plush black velvet blazer and skirt that a woman in the church had given me. "Elegant," I decided, "and delightfully slimming." I think I was still unconsciously reluctant to allow myself to look pregnant. A shimmery gold bow-tied blouse completed the outfit. Examining my reflection in the mirror, I was pleased with the clothes, but they didn't help perk up my pale face or erase the circles under my eyes. "More blush," I decided. "If people think I look white now, they should see my without my blush." I laughed.

My hair was another story. It sadly needed some attention that I obviously hadn't given it lately. It looked like the hanging moss on our oak trees outside. With my curling iron in hand, I attacked the mass and pushed the brownish blonde locks into place. Pulling together the mid-length hair in the back, I smoothed it into a modified french twist and gingerly fastened it with a hair comb. Patting the final strands into place, another glance in the mirror brought my approval. "I may look like an elegant woman, ready to tackle anything, but first impressions aren't always true," I cajoled.

Sometimes people would confess to me their first impressions of my character. They were sure I was self-confident and maybe even conceited. This always upset me. Inwardly, I was totally the opposite. I felt pressure to be friendly and outgoing because I married a pastor; but many times, I yearned to sit down and say nothing. People found it difficult to believe I was shy. I found "small talk" frustrating. God's strength enabled me to push myself, yielding my desires and intentions into His hands.

Smoothing the wrinkles from the velvet skirt, I

sighed and determined to struggle through the candlelight service. "They'll never know how scared and depressed I am. I wish I could find a safe hole to hide in."

The dimly lit sanctuary provided a perfect cover for me. The low light made a good screen. I knew if anyone looked too closely they would see a dam of tears ready to burst. I chose the fourth pew from the front and eased into the padded red seat slowly. The deep oak wood gave ample support to my faltering frame. Holly and David plopped down next to me while I held squirming Jonathan. More and more people quietly stepped into the hushed sanctuary. The kids fidgeted, thoughts of Christmas presents pricking their bodies into unrest. I refrained from eye contact with people, fearing my response to the slightest look of concern. "I've got to keep cool through this service," I reminded myself.

Jonathan grew more and more restless. I found the combination of wrestling with him and keeping a lid on my emotions horribly draining. He sensed my tiredness. I handed him to Phil's sister, Judell. "Please hold him for me. I can't handle him tonight."

Again, I found refuge in the pew. I glanced to my right and viewed my friend Diane sitting down. She looked glowing in her pink maternity dress. Her long blonde hair swept the neckline. Her skin bloomed with color. "Boy, what a difference between us," I thought.

I recalled the day she revealed her condition to me. I went home from Sunday morning church early, feeling slightly sick. I put Jonathan to bed and rested on our blue and gold striped couch. The family's noon meal was on my mind. "I need to get up and muster something."

"Can I come in?" a voice from the screen door called. Peeking around the corner, I saw Diane with her young son, Keith.

"Sure," I answered, "if you can stand the mess." I was embarrassed. The Sunday paper was scattered everywhere. Dishes were in the sink. Clothes stayed where the kids dropped them.

"I saw you come home and since Keith wasn't feeling so well, I thought I'd walk over and visit with you. I hope you don't mind," she asked questioningly.

"No, don't worry about it. Come on in." I signaled with my hand.

She lowered herself onto our blue tweed footstool.

"Hey, Di, guess what? I just found out I'm pregnant. I'm so excited I can hardly stand it. I must be crazy or something, but I really want another child." Her son squirmed in her arms like a wrestler being pinned. I noticed her downcast eyes and silence. Her thin face revealed a sadness I hadn't noticed earlier. Her brown eyes met my scrutinizing look.

"I'm pretty sure I'm pregnant, too, but I guess I'm not as happy about it as you are."

I searched for words to express my empathy and understanding. I realized she was speaking from tiredness. She already had two children under four and little Keith was just eleven months old. She was still in a state of shock. This child had been planned by God, not by them.

After a few moments of sharing the joys and trials of children we compared "due dates." According to our calculations, our babies would be born possibly days apart. I was thrilled to have a "pregnant partner" and tried to lift her spirits further. I made a mental note of this and determined to give her occasional calls, encouragement and help down our shared road. Maybe it would lighten her load.

The memory of that encounter faded as I surveyed Diane tonight, December 24th, and shook those daydreams from my mind. The sanctuary was almost filled to capacity now and only the buzzing of whispered conversations were heard.

Diane searched my face. "How are you?" she mouthed silently across the room.

Reading her lips, I shook my head back and forth to signal a negative response. A lump of emotion rose in my throat as I gave a "thumbs down" gesture. Through her glasses her eyes saddened. She gave me a doe-eyed look of concern.

Quickly I turned my head toward the front. I wanted to divert my thoughts to something else. I choked back the tears, refusing to give in to my sadness.

Soon music filled the air. Jubilantly we sang "Joy To The World" and "Hark The Herald Angels Sing," "Silent Night" and "Away In A Manger." I couldn't participate fully. Every time I came across the word "baby" I twinged. The sweet lullabies brought pain instead of comfort. "Oh if only I could forget all this," I cried.

The remainder of the short service was vague to me. My thoughts were a million miles away. Moment after moment I struggled to shove all my problems out. But I was weary from this continual battle and I resigned myself to fight it no longer. As scripture was read and the service continued, I allowed myself moments of agonizing grief. The loss of my two babies through miscarriage was very real to me. "Lord, I never saw their faces, but I know you see them now. How I long to cradle them in my arms." Confused, I asked, "How can I feel grief over someone I've never known?" This question whizzed through my mind repeatedly.

Fear again became my unwelcome advisor and echoed sadistically, "Your baby's going to die tomorrow, tomorrow. Then you'll have none left. Your baby's going to die, die, die." Nervous perspiration dripped from my face. With the lighting of our individual candles, the warm glow grew in intensity as the light passed from person to person. The task completed, we listened as a final prayer was said and in unison all candles were extinguished. The sanctuary lights came on. I moved out quickly and with a weak smile headed for the door. My emotions were ready to spill. I couldn't hold them much longer. I needed to release the tears as desperately as I depended on breathing.

I wasn't quick enough. One woman caught me and asked, "How are you doing?" Her clear green eyes fixed on my face and seemed to penetrate to my soul. I was losing composure and she sensed it.

"Oh, I'm hanging in there," I found myself hypocritically answering. But this rehearsed pat answer didn't cloak sufficiently. Tears immediately welled up and spilled out.

Being only a few steps from the exit door, she gathered me discreetly in her sure arms and guided me outside into the privacy of a darkened hallway. I leaned against the white plaster wall for strength, gasped for air and set free the remaining flood of tears. She wrapped her arms around me and stroked my back.

"Oh, I'm so scared," I confided.

She listened sympathetically. She took her unspoken cue and sensed I needed to cry and verbalize all my pent-up emotions. I confessed my superstitious feelings of fear about the trip to my parents. I expressed my tiredness, my grief and the numbness of the whole Christmas season.

She patiently waited for the right moment and then applied her special balm of encouragement. She reminded me of God's promise while not ignoring the physical part of my trial. That ugly, vile fear slithered away and was replaced once again by serenity.

I mustered up strength, wiped my eyes and thanked

her for being such a special friend. She whispered a prayer and then helped me into our car. I assured her I would be all right and she left, reminding me of her prayers on the morrow, Christmas Day.

Phil opened the door and slipped into the driver's seat. His tender eyes met my glance and he knew something had happened. He waited for me to explain. I loved him for many reasons and his patience was one of them.

My emotional encounter revealed, he searched for my hand in the moonlit darkness and gave it a gentle squeeze. I leaned sideways and placed my arms around his strong shoulders.

8
December 25

After a fitful night's sleep, I reluctantly crawled out of bed and began my preparations for the big day ahead. Phil awakened our sleepy-eyed children and helped them open their presents. Each package brought a squeal of delight or wide-eyed approval. Wrapping paper and boxes littered the floor, blonde heads poking from underneath.

Phil took charge and quickly gave Jonathan his morning bath. Holly and David proudly modeled their new Christmas outfits and waited as I brushed my teeth. As we ushered our little ones into the car in the predawn darkness, I closed the door hesitantly, wondering what would transpire during this day.

Childish chatter faded into sleepy silence. The steady hum of whirring tires filled the car with a lullaby symphony.

I closed my eyes and drifted into a light sleep. Awakened, my odometer brain clicked off the miles to the infamous gas station. Flashbacks of blood, dirt and horror unsettled me. My eyes searched for comfort from Phil. He placed his hand over mine and squeezed with steady, firm pressure. My grip tightened.

There it was, the gas station, darkened, with only the morning dawn illuminating the dreaded premises. It quickly faded from view as we sped by. Tensed muscles relaxed in response to the long-waited relief.

"Well, Honey, I made it," I whispered, breaking the silence.

"I know, Hon. Now you can lay back and get some rest. I knew you wouldn't really sleep until we passed this point in the road. Everything's all right now, isn't it?" he questioned.

"Yes, I can't believe all that's happened in six days. It seems so much longer. Six days ago, when I left that gas station, I never dreamed I would still have the baby. Isn't God good!" I relaxed in the seat. Victory from facing my superstitious fears excited me. Fear had poisoned my Christmas, but with the Lord's strength I had passed this hurdle and won.

Though nausea and weakness still plagued me, I enjoyed the relaxing pace of the remaining day. Precious family moments were again relived. The two hour return trip was filled with praise and thanks to God for the gift of this special Christmas Day.

Christmas was now a week-old memory. The heavier bleeding lessened and the continual spotting became commonplace. I had little strength for anything, so Phil and the kids pitched in and struggled with my tasks.

By New Year's Eve I was still too weak to attend our annual Watchnight Service. Television and books were my companions. I got into bed and fought for sleep.

Things began to settle down and I hesitatingly allowed myself optimistic thoughts of the future. Surviving the holidays took a great deal of energy but I did survive. Other things now seemed easier in comparison.

We slowly began to get back into the normal flow of life. The kids' vacation time was over and they were back in school again. Food began to smell good to me once more, so eating was a renewed interest. Although the hard pounding of jogging was now definitely ruled out, brisk walking was my next choice.

By January 9th my physical stamina was renewed. "Sue, you have that becoming pregnant glow," a parishioner commented. In some ways the three month mark in my pregnancy was hard to fathom. The crucial first trimester was almost over.

Staring at the simulated bamboo wall covering in the doctor's office, I waited for Ann to enter. The white door swung open, revealing a short woman with close-cropped brown hair. She was the other midwife who shared duty with Lynne. Her calm demeanor pleased me. Ann was not the type to get easily ruffled. In her soft-spoken way she asked me how I was feeling.

"I'm hanging in there," was my well-rehearsed reply.

"Have you had any more bleeding?" she asked as her brown eyes scanned my chart.

With some excitement, I almost cockily answered, "No! Would you believe I've had nothing since New Year's Eve? I'm really encouraged."

Her eyebrows lifted in surprise. A small, not too wide grin flashed from her mouth. "Really Sue? That's great! Who knows? Maybe you'll get through this after all."

Her expression of optimism was brief. The smile vanished and was replaced with a somber look. "You've still got those other two sacs in there though," she reminded. "So you still need to be careful."

"Oh, I will," I assured. "But I personally think that the worst is over."

Not wanting to dampen my spirits, Ann added, "I sure hope so, Sue." She reached for the dopler and placed the cold metal on my tummy.

"If only they'd give me some encouragement," I thought. "I know they don't want to give me false hopes, but I sure get tired of their reserve. I wish they could just say, 'You're fine. The worst is all over. From now on you'll have a totally normal pregnancy.'" In my heart, though, I knew they were right. I could fantasize positive things all I wanted, but it still didn't change the realities of my condition.

Once again, we listened to the baby's rapid, thumping heartbeat. Ann's nod and smile assured me that at least the heartbeat seemed normal. The quick rhythm was music to my ears and renewed my hope the baby would survive his ordeal.

After Ann's departure, I changed my clothes. The flower of hope bloomed into larger glory. Flinging back the curtain from the dressing booth, I tried to set free any nagging doubts. I offered a silent prayer. "Oh Lord, please let me have a normal pregnancy from now on." These last three months had seemed like the longest of my life. I wanted the remaining months to be blissfully free of complications.

The appointment desk was my next stop. I had to schedule next week's visit. Another sonogram was also on the agenda. We couldn't wait to see how much the baby had grown.

The view that flashed across the ultrasound screen on January 17 was better than an Oscar-winning movie. For the first time I could actually see the baby's entire shape. Feet and legs moved freely and that precious heart was rhythmically thumping. Psalm 139 verse 14 flashed across my mind: "I praise you because I am fearfully and wonderfully made." We saw delicate, uniform ribs as the baby's active form turned from side to side.

I saw a welcome smile on Jessie's lips. "The baby looks real good, Sue. There's quite a bit of movement which is a good sign."

Phil reached out and touched my cold ankle as if he could transmit his feelings. He could hardly contain his excitement and awe. We relished every minute of our top-rated TV show, starring Engelman number four.

Lynne briskly stepped in. For a moment her casual demeanor cracked as she voiced what we all felt. "It's really somethin', isn't it? I mean, to be able to get a peek into God's workshop?"

How I thanked God for endowing men with the intelligence to bring us this technology. In those awesome and very personal moments, God allowed His curtain to be rolled back. We beheld one of His continual miracles. Baby performed his graceful ballet to the beat of his favorite sound, our hearts, together thumping a melodical symphony. Every tiny movement proclaimed God's glory and entranced us all. Time was momentarily put into slow motion as all of us were silent spectators to this drama of the universe.

Jessie froze the picture on the screen in order to measure the baby's head and femur bone. She was trying to determine the baby's specific fetal age. According to all charts, this little beauty was now fifteen and a half weeks old.

I searched for the other two sacs. "I hope they're gone," I silently wished. Like unwanted pests I spied what I thought were the sacs.

Soon another doctor stepped into our darkened room. By now the whole clinic was anxious to know what the outcome would be in the wierd Engelman case.

Lynne pointed out the sacs, but noted they looked smaller in size. As Jessie showed other angles, someone asked for a view of the placenta.

Silence. "Is all that the placenta?" the doctor asked, trying to hide her surprise.

Lynne explained her triplet theory. They nodded in agreement that triplets would best explain the enormous, bulky placenta we were seeing. Even the connecting blood vessels were larger in size.

"Yes," Lynne explained, "it looks as though your body made definite preparations for more than one baby."

The show over, everyone exited. Phil and I embraced as we mentally replayed all we had witnessed.

The examination room beckoned us welcomingly. It no longer seemed cold and sterile. As Lynne stepped in the room, I revealed my well-thought-out theory about my situation.

"You see, I think all this bleeding is coming from those two sacs and once they are gone everything will be fine. You just wait and see. Before long, I won't be coming in here every week. You'll have to see me only once a month and I'll get fat and sassy and normal!"

Giving her typical half-grin, she replied, "I sure hope so, Sue. At this stage of the game, you know about as much as we do. I wish I could give you a positive answer but...."

"Only God knows," we chimed in unison, repeating our favorite phrase.

Leaving the office, I whispered a prayer, "Dear Lord, if it be your will, please get rid of these two empty sacs so I can be normal." Little did I know the significance of that prayer or the swiftness with which it would be answered.

The following days yielded more and more peace and feelings of well-being. I went to the local thrift store and allowed myself the luxury of looking at maternity clothes. I even bought a pretty white top with blue hearts all over. My optimistic plans were to wear it on Valentine's Day for Phil. With a more positive outlook, I cautiously began a modified exercise routine. Someone in the church gave us a rebounder (small round trampoline), and I decided I would use it to gradually ease into some gentle exercise. We purchased a baby seat for my bike and soon Jonathan's white-blond hair was flying as we took rides around the neighborhood.

One evening, while resting in the solace of my bed, I laid my hand on my abdomen to give the baby his good night tap. As my fingers rested, I felt upward pressure on my hand. Thrilled by the sensation, I removed my hand. My eyes were glued to my stomach. Seconds passed, and then a quarter-sized lump rapidly rose and fell. My suspicions were correct. The baby had moved and blessed me with a good night tap of his own.

Days ticked by a little quicker. Every day seemed like another victory as it passed trouble-free. I felt better all the time and with nearly one trouble-free month behind me I was beginning to feel like my old self.

9
"Get Her To The Hospital"

"Hi, Cheryl. Come on in." It was Wednesday and time for our half-hour workout. Cheryl methodically rolled her silver rebounder into the living room and started to screw the legs into place. Her pale blue leotard coaxed even more color from her strikingly sky-blue eyes. Fixing a terry headband in place over her blonde hair, she stooped and casually slipped on matching blue legwarmers and ballet slippers.

Everything about Cheryl was casual. The day she delivered her son Ned, I phoned her in the hospital. I asked how she felt and what the labor was like.

"Oh...fine," she matter-of-factly answered.

"Oh, uh, how's the baby?"

"Oh...fine," answering with low-keyed enthusiasm.

Another pause. I searched for something else to say. She wasn't one for wordy phone conversations.

"Well," I fumbled, "uh...glad everything went so well. We're really happy for you. We're praying for you. See you later."

Gratefully hanging up the phone, I chuckled. I felt I had just held a conversation with someone who finished taking a stroll around the corner. Certainly the conversation typified her easy-going character. To her, labor was just no big deal.

I often teased her about her steady, even keel. I needed someone like that, especially now, and I was thankful to claim her as my friend.

We stepped on our rebounders as the record started playing. Cheryl insisted I was merciless when it came to exercise because I never gave her a break to rest. As the music played on, my pulse increased. I noticed I was more tired than usual. Pulling my legs up was more difficult. Physically I felt different. Mental alarm bells signalled and suddenly that sickening "rush" came again.

Running from the room, I prayed what I suspected wasn't true. My heart plummeted. More bleeding. Tears burst from the deep caverns where I'd pushed them and fell into fresh flows.

Music ceased in the living room. I knew Cheryl wondered what happened. Mustering my strength, I walked into the room and faced Cheryl's questioning gaze. The tears painted their story on my flushed cheeks. "I'm bleeding again. Oh, why, why can't this stop? I'm so afraid."

Cheryl rushed to comfort me as I fell into the chair.

"Maybe I shouldn't have exercised today." Quietly and in self-defense I justified my actions by saying, "But if my exercise was hurting the baby, wouldn't the bleeding have started weeks ago when I carefully began this?"

Smoothing my sweaty hair, Cheryl answered, "Sue, you've done the best you can. You're just going to have to trust God with this."

It was just what I needed to hear in that moment. She could say those words to me because she knew me well enough and cared. Her true scriptural advice had been covered in love and concern. That's what mattered most.

"Do you want me to call Phil and have him come

home?"

A new knot twisted in my stomach as I thought of breaking the news to Phil. We had both allowed our hopes to grow beyond previous boundaries. Each day we spoke of the baby in more personal terms. Phil had fallen in love with this very special "fighter."

"No," I answered. "I'll tell him later when he comes home for lunch."

Cheryl left reluctantly as I assured her I would be okay. Again I sat alone in the house, staring at the walls. A feeling in the pit of my stomach told me this was the dread beginning of a whole new ball game.

The bleeding eased, but I never stepped on the rebounder again. Weakness set in. I found my well-worn spot on the living room couch during the days and Phil and the kids reassumed their new household duties.

It was February 11, the night of our Missionary Banquet and I was determined to go no matter what. It seemed an eternity since I had attended a regular church function. With the bleeding slowed, I felt it was relatively safe to walk the fifty yards from our house to the church fellowship hall.

I wondered if I could hold up through both the meal and the meeting. Getting dressed was a major challenge. With each activity, the bleeding increased. Deep down, warning signals were going off, but I suppressed them and kept going.

The Fellowship Hall was alive with festive colors and jam-packed with people. I held off my arrival until the last few minutes so I wouldn't have to engage in lengthy conversations. Phil was cordial and passed his electric smile and humble greetings to several individuals as we were seated.

Holly and David wanted to sit with their friends but I insisted they stay with me. Phil had to take care of several things, so I needed the kids for my support and company. David squirmed unhappily in his seat. Holly's piercing blue eyes bore holes into me. Her tiny features, normally so fragile and lovely, squinched together in a scowl as she rested her chin on her hands. I gave her my "you better straighten up or else" stare and her scowl softened a little.

The caterers were busily getting food uncovered. People scurried to get in their seats so Phil could open in prayer. Everyone was ready to eat. My appetite was surprisingly large and all the food looked so enticing. As we took our place in the buffet line, panic struck. I felt another surge. Was I going to be able to stay?

Turning my thoughts inward, I counseled myself. "You'll be all right. Just hurry and get your food. You haven't been up for a while and that's probably why you're bleeding."

"Pray for me, Hon," I whispered to Phil. "It's started again."

His calm expression changed. Nervously he adjusted his glasses and asked, "Are you sure you want to stay?"

I confided my doubts, but still wanted to try and remain at the banquet at least through the rest of the meal. My hunger pangs left and I picked at the food. Nothing appealed to me. The potatoes seemed bland, the green beans overdone and the chicken too greasy. I managed to consume a polite amount and decided to go back for something that might suit my tastes better.

Pushing to a crouching position, I leaned toward Phil.

"Honey," I whispered, "you better check the back of my dress." His face turned white. "Don't get up, Hon," he insisted.

"You're kidding, am I bleeding that badly?" His affirmative nod answered my question. My thoughts scrambled. How could I gracefully exit without anyone seeing my obvious distress?

Fortunately, we sat at the far end of the hall, close to an accordian room divider. On the other side of the divider was an empty room and an exit that faced our house. We developed a plan of action. I would stand up, back up against the wooden divider and pretend to be carrying on a conversation with Phil. People didn't even notice our exit and soon Phil spirited me out the door. If the situation hadn't been so serious I would've laughed.

It was a beautiful moonlit night. The air was crisp but not too cool. Muffled buzzzing of people's conversations could be heard as the brisk clop clop of my heels hit the cement and echoed into the still night air. My heart raced. With every step more surges flowed. "Is it bad, Hon? Do the spots on my dress look big?"

"It's...it's kind of hard to tell in the dark, but it looks pretty bad."

The dam of tears was building. Fear wretched my soul. Panic seized me as I ran to our bathroom. Tossing my outfit aside into the shower, Phil grabbed a change of clothing. His horror stricken eyes met mine.

"Oh Lord!" I gasped, "I'm losing the baby! Oh Honey, I'm so scared. I can't lose the baby now. Everything was going so well!" Tears choked out any remaining words. I began to hyperventilate as fear unleashed its fury. The very core of my soul convulsed.

Phil helped me into bed. Everything started spinning. My head felt like a feather and I knew black out was near. I struggled to slow my breathing and calm my emotions. Regaining some composure, I instructed, "Phil, would you give me the phone so I can call the midwife?"

He handed me the phone. "Honey, I have to go back to the Fellowship Hall and let people know what's happening. Do you want me to get someone to stay with you while I make some arrangements?"

Emotions clouded any clear thinking. "No...I mean, yes. I guess you better have someone come." Marilyn's smiling face flashed across my mind. "Get Marilyn, okay?"

He nodded and ran out the door. I dialed the emergency number and spoke to Ann. The sound of her voice released more tears. Somehow I managed to describe the situation and the amount of bleeding. Our conversation ended as she seriously instructed, "Get down here to the hospital right away."

Marilyn arrived and swept into action with decisiveness and wisdom. Her brown curls flipping, she set to work elevating my feet. Her previous medical experience came in handy. "Slow down, Sue. Slow that breathing down. Don't worry. We'll take care of you. Everything's under control. I'm going to get you in the car and take you to the hospital. Phil will meet us down there as soon as he gets the meeting started." Her strength calmed me.

Moving to the edge of the bed, I sensed another surge. "Grab me a towel, Marilyn, I'm going to need it."

She knew the rising panic and continued to assertively calm me down. I slid slowly into her car as she reclined the front seat and stuffed towels and pillows underneath my legs.

Speeding down the highway, I thought about the possible conclusion of this hospital visit and my legs began to shake. This wasn't the time or way I had planned to go. I needed something to calm me and asked Marilyn if we could sing some hymns.

Weakly sung, yet full of emotion, the words from "It Is Well With My Soul" poured forth from our lips.

When peace like a river attendeth my way

76

When sorrows like sea billows roll
Whatever my lot, Thou hast taught me to say
It is well, it is well with my soul.

I blinked back tears while I shakily joined Marilyn in the chorus of "Count Your Many Blessings."

The quivering intensified and my teeth chattered from an imagined chill. Marilyn threw a towel over me, but nothing warmed the shaking fear. "Why can't I stop my body from doing this?" My protruding tummy tightened in a familiar way. A cramp? I checked my watch. Two minutes later the muscles tightened again. Sickening fear squeezed me. Another two minutes and another pain. I didn't want to admit it, but I knew I was in mild labor. As fear threw a black curtain over my mind, I fought to throw it back.

I searched for Marilyn's hand in the silence and squeezed. "Marilyn...I'm in labor...." Admitting it helped lift some of the fear.

Concern twisted her youthful face and instantaneously added lines. She burst into prayer. "Oh dear Lord, please help my sister, Sue. She loves You so, Lord, and she needs your calming touch. Please keep this baby safe and if it's Your will, please stop her bleeding and her labor pains. In Jesus' Name, Amen."

The corners of my lips slowly turned upward and I thanked Marilyn as we pulled up to the emergency entrance of the hospital. Gathering up all my towels, I flopped myself into a wheelchair. The finger-smudged silver doors mechanically opened with a buzz as we entered the emergency area. Hearing the buzz again, I turned and my eyes filled with the welcome picture of my handsome husband. He really did look the part of a preacher tonight, The conservatively stylish blue suit fit perfectly. His white shirt, contrasted against his patterned tie, completed his crisp, neat lines. His ruddy cheeks seemed drained of their usual color as he tenderly brushed his hand against my shoulder.

"You doing okay?"

"Yes. But I'm awfully scared and my legs keep shaking. I'm so cold."

Dutifully he rushed and asked a nurse for a blanket. She brought a toasty white fleece blanket and wrapped it around my knocking knees.

As we waited to be admitted, people curiously watched. Their glances falling on my swollen tummy brought slow smiles to their lips. I surmised what they were thinking. I reacted inwardly. "I'm here too soon, you silly people. If only you knew why I'm here."

Nurses briskly walked to their destinations. The droneful voice of a woman paging a doctor interrupted the silence. My eyes turned to other figures slouched in the gray metal chairs. Their hollow eyes reflected worry, some pain. I turned to remove them from my vision and stared at my cold toes. "I've got enough pain of my own without seeing theirs," I sighed.

A young brown-haired girl walked toward my wheelchair. Her blue patterned frock reminded me she was from the third floor of labor and delivery.

Handing me a clip board, she asked me to sign the admittance and consent form. The beige-speckled tiles disappeared under my wheelchair. The ugly green walls flashed by my view as we travelled down the long hall to get to the elevator and third floor. Newly-installed blue-gray carpet matched pleasingly with the recently painted blue-gray walls.

Whizzing into another corridor she intructed Phil and Marilyn. "Will you two please wait here in the lobby? We'll check back with you in a bit."

Helplessly glancing back, my eyes said goodbye to Phil. Memories flooded in as we entered the labor and delivery area. Was it only a year and a half ago when

I was here to give birth to our joy-baby, Jonathan? I recognized a couple of the nurses.

I was wheeled into the small labor admittance room. Its low lights didn't hide all the equipment. Two high hospital beds hugged opposite walls, petitioned off by a muslin curtain.

Lynne managed a weak smile as she snapped on a surgical glove. "C'mon, Sue. Hop up here and let's see what's goin' on." She patted the white sheets.

The rising movement brought another surge. I quickly crouched and grabbed the towel. "I think I'll need some help, Lynne." More twinges came and the bed loomed above me like the Empire State Building.

"That's okay, Sue. Let's get you up here." She and a nurse smoothly assisted me.

Once on the bed, more pains seized me, stronger in intensity. A not-so-comforting sensation of leaking fluid hit. "My water just broke, didn't it?" I asked with a lump in my throat.

All the jokes and silly glances were absent now from Lynne's face. The gaiety in her blue eyes gone, her concern was obvious. "Yes, Sue, your membranes have ruptured." The attending nurse nodded in agreement as Lynne prodded through her tasks.

Lynne observed my flinch and placed her hand softly on my tightening tummy muscles. "You're having another contraction, aren't you? That one felt pretty strong. Are they getting closer together?"

Tears replaced my words and I simply nodded in agreement. I childishly hoped I could hide my labor from her. I felt the quickening of my child's movements and drew some comfort that life was still there. How could this be happening to me? I was angry that I couldn't control my body and force it to stop what it was doing. This horrid nightmare grew worse and more real every day. I squeezed my eyes tightly shut as if blinking would make me wake up into a better world. "Oh Lord, I wanted this baby so badly. I've tried so hard. Is this how it's going to end?" I thought.

"I think we need to get a fetal monitor on her. We'll see how the baby's handling all this." Lynne spoke as she and the nurse exited to retrieve the machine. I heard groans of pain from a laboring woman down the hall. As her cries intensified they soon ceased and were replaced with the high squalls of a newborn child.

The cries stabbed me with pain. I felt an intruder had rushed into my room and menacingly played on the whole birthing scene before my eyes. My imagined, invisible pest put that sweet newborn babe next to my ears and let the lusty cries roll, piercing me to the core of my soul.

He laughed sadistically. "This isn't how it will be with you, Sue." he sneered. "Your baby's too young— you'll never, ever, hear his cry. He'll die and his cries will be smothered by me, Death. Ha, ha, ha, ha, ha. You can't help it. I will steal your child from your womb early. He's going to die, die die!"

I wrestled to free myself from this torturous scene in my mind and willfully stopped the thoughts.

"When peace like a river attendeth my way, when sorrows like sea billows roll," I sang weakly, tears choking out the melody. This song melted into other hymns as I regained composure from God. I felt instantly buoyed. My spirits were soaring and a rising crescendo of God's grace-filled song ministered to the searing pain in my soul. As I finished my impromptu concert, Phil and Lynne entered.

Phil's grave expression told me Lynne had filled him in on my condition. His strong hand reached for mine and squeezed it tightly. He conjured up a forced smile and stroked my tousled hair, pushing away strands from my tear-stained eyes. Though he tried to disguise it, I could feel his hand tremble as I held it.

Lowering her eyes, Lynne shuffled uneasily next to us. Clearing her throat, she said, "Sue, I don't think there's much chance you're going to keep this baby." Silence clung to her ending sentence as she pensively folded her arms and looked at us.

"I guess God answered my prayer," I interrupted. "Just the other day, when I was in your office, I prayed that He would get rid of these extra sacs, if it was His will. Do you think I just lost the extra sacs, or did I lose the sac around the baby too?"

Forcing the unwelcome information from her lips, I waited her response. "Sue, I think you're right to pray. I also think that you better pray now and ask God to get this thing over with quickly. I'm not sure if the baby's sac was ruptured, but I doubt if it's intact. Most likely when the other two sacs left, they pulled free, leaving a hole in the baby's sac. I've got no pat answers. We'll just have to wait and see."

"You mean you think she's going to lose the baby?" Phil questioned. "She still feels the baby kicking," he added defensively.

"I don't think there's much hope at this point," Lynne solemnly replied. "When you first came in your cervix was tight and closed, a sign that the contractions weren't doing anything. But when I checked you just now, the cervix was beginning to soften. You could begin to dilate soon."

All hope washed from me as she uttered her last words. Exhaustion flooded in as my emotions fought for a release. The blue walls gave no comfort. They only echoed my dullness of mind. The world that closed in on me was all labeled "blue."

10
"The Kid Is A Fighter"

I'll leave you two alone for a while and check back with you in a bit."

As Lynne exited, Phil slumped into my arms. I felt the slow drip of hot tears falling on my skin. We whispered tender, moving prayers as our hearts joined in unison asking God to spare our little fighter if it was His will. We also asked that things would happen quickly if I was to lose the baby. I was afraid of a long drawn-out process full of pain and a slow death for the baby.

I was moved to one of the labor and delivery rooms to begin our waiting vigil. Lynne said she would stay at the hospital a while and check on my progress. The small quiet room was free of any distractions. I longed to hook my mind onto other thoughts. I wanted to block out the noise of the "blessed events" continually interrupting my silence. My exhaustion and lack of food was taking its toll. Had I not been in bed, I would've been too weak to sit up. An IV was started with glucose to keep up my strength. Phil snatched some fitful sleep in a chair next to my bed.

I stared at the walls, then at the ceiling, then at the crisp clean sheets hiding my swollen tummy. Phil had shed his preacherly garb and merely gave the appearance of a weary father-in-waiting. The slightest sound awakened him, so I tried not to stir. Nurses tiptoed in, got my vital signs and checked on my contractions.

One lamp cast soft shadows over the room. My thoughts slowed and were replaced with a growing heaviness. This could be my child's birthday. Each kick reminded me our little fighter was still trying. Oh how I'd grown to love this unseen part of me. Our attachments were so strong. How I wished he would remain in his soft, warm world. But my hope had gone. I knew I was going to lose him. "Oh Lord," I whispered, "I'm so disappointed. So tired, oh Lord...."

Minute after agonizing minute passed. Phil nuzzled a pillow and slept on the cold floor. My contractions seemed to be slowing. Hours passed and still no more pains. Had the contractions completely stopped? I was confused. Was I disappointed that everything quit? I was so tired; I wouldn't allow myself a glimmer of hope. Phil awakened and asked about the contractions. He grew more encouraged as contraction-free hours passed. I felt numb and wanted everything settled. I didn't want any more in-between phases.

It was obvious nothing more was going to happen for a while. Lynne checked me, "Sue, nothin's gonna happen for a while. I'll go home and come back in the morning."

The nurses instructed, "Go ahead and try to get some rest, Sue." I convinced Phil to go home and pick up some things for me. He needed some rest. He reluctantly agreed and his tired frame shuffled out and down the hall.

The bleeding dwindled to nothing as all contractions ceased. Every half-hour or so they checked the baby's heartbeat and it just got stronger and stronger. I fought back the seed of hope which stubbornly started growing again. If only I could push it out of my heart. Why couldn't I be detached and unfeeling? I resented the hurt that followed hope and I was tired of being on this sickening emotional seesaw.

The horrid Friday slowly faded forever and Saturday's rosy fingers of dawn crept into my room. I watched the whole process from my bed as sleep eluded me. Phil appeared, looking a little more rested, his face echoing apprehension. "Still no contractions?"

"No," I responded, "and my bleeding has completely stopped." A smile spread across his face. "Honey, maybe everything will be all right after all. Last night, Marilyn told me they started an all night prayer vigil for you. I think maybe the Lord has answered prayer."

"Well, let's not get our hopes up too soon," I cautiously warned. "We still don't know if the baby's membranes have ruptured. Maybe they'll do a sonogram this morning."

Several hours passed and soon Lynne's face appeared at my bedside. She examined me and found I hadn't dilated. She didn't look jubilant. I didn't know what I was reading in her expression. "Sue, one of the doctors from the clinic will come in soon and see you. I think she'll want another sonogram so we know for sure what happened. It seems your labor has completely stopped and you've had no dilation. I still don't know if the baby's sac ruptured or not." She reached for my white hand and gave it a squeeze.

"Well, she's made it this far. Maybe the baby's going to make it," Phil exclaimed.

"I know one thing, this kid sure is a fighter," Lynne acknowledged. Concern flashed across her eyes. "How are you holdin' up, Sue? I know this is a real ordeal. How are you handling things?"

"I'm so tired. I don't know what to think. I'm afraid to let myself hope because I don't want to be disappointed again. But I do know this, if God wants this baby to live, he'll survive no matter what. As tired as I am, I want God's will before mine. He'll give me the strength to get through this. We want to do everything we possibly can to save this baby."

"Well, I told the doctors, if anyone can handle this, you guys can," Lynne added, patting my hand and straightening the covers. "I'll be thinkin' of ya. I'll check in on you later, after the doctor's seen you."

Each time she left, so did some of my confidence. Ever since Lynne delivered our son Jonathan, I felt a strong attachment to her. I realized how many emotions intertwined and mysteriously bonded us together in an unspoken friendship. Sharing a happy birthing event cemented a tender feeling in my heart that nothing could ever loose. I was saddened at the not-so-happy prospects of this delivery. I wondered if she felt some of these things or if she had learned to become emotionally detached.

The heaviness was again pressing in on me. I was too tired to cry and afraid to think for fear I would build more hope.

"Honey, could you get out my radio and turn it to Keswick?" I knew hearing the hymns would soothe me. We spent the next few moments drinking in strength from the words of favorite hymns and scripture readings on the Christian radio station.

A tall, attractive blonde came around to my left side. Her slim face and figure completed her pleasing appearance. She smiled warmly as she opened my chart and patted my hand. "Hello, Sue. I'm Dr. Benson. Looks as if you've had a really rough night, but you seem to be doing well now. We'd like to get another sonogram." I was startled by her friendliness and lack of the typical doctor's sterility. Phil and I both welcomed this change.

The nurse brought a filled glass and I sipped the

water as quickly as possible. Emotions and hunger had twisted my stomach into a queasy mess and the water didn't help. Soon it was time to go. Dr. Benson, Phil and a nurse pushed my bed down the hall and into a waiting elevator. We stared silently at the flashing numbers and the doors swished open. "Lord," I uttered silently, "I'm so scared. I feel so helpless. Please give me strength to go on."

Building anticipation and the cold air blowing on me produced nervous twitching in my legs. I struggled to stop it.

The technician again greeted us. Phil breathed a sigh of relief when they didn't question his presence. We'd been told he might have to wait in another room. As the cold jelly splatted on my tummy, goose bumps appeared. No one spoke as the image became visible on the screen.

"Here's the baby's head and there's the heart." I was relieved to see it still beating. No extra sacs were visible. There seemed to be no bleeding from the placenta. "So far, so good," I thought. According to the measurements and pictures, baby was dated at 19 weeks. As the technician finished taking more measurements and pictures, Phil and I turned toward Dr. Benson. We asked for her explanations.

Another doctor had been called in and they both decided that things looked pretty good. "There is some decrease in the amniotic fluid around the baby, which could mean there is a small hole somewhere. We can't see one in the sonogram. If it's just a small hole, it may heal and you could be fine. If it's loo large, it cannot heal and you would contiue to lose amniotic fluid. But considering your case," a wry smile crossed her lips, "we'll give you the benefit of the doubt."

Again I fought back disbelief. Another miracle God had performed. I was awestruck that He had brought my baby and me through the night. Dr. Benson continued.

"I really would rather keep you in the hospital, but I know this is an expensive hotel. Lynne explained to me that you have plenty of help at home. There are several things you must do or I can't let you leave. The risk of infection is high now, so you must take your temperature every four hours. You're going to have to stay flat in bed for at least a week until we check your progress at the office."

I hated the thought of being confined to bed but promised to do so if it would save the baby. She wished us luck and told us we could go home.

Before 10 a.m. that same Saturday, Phil excitedly pushed me in the wheelchair out the glass doors of the hospital. Gingerly easing into the seat of our Honda, I lay back, breathing a sigh of relief as my hand tenderly patted my swollen tummy. Though I was exhausted, inwardly my emotions were bursting into explosions of happiness.

My grin widened as I included Phil in my thoughts. "Honey, can you believe we've still got this baby? What a miracle!"

"I can hardly wait to see the looks on people's faces," he added.

As our car buzzed home, I examined the world passing by my right window. Familiar buildings stood in the same places, landscape unchanged, but everything seemed sharp, clean and pleasant. The sky burst a brighter blue, with pure white clouds completing the colorful horizon. Phil found a way to drive the car close to our front doorstep.

Managing to still my dizzy head, I slowly reached for Phil's outstretched arm as he assisted me. Every muscle in my body ached and the brief walk from the car to our bedroom was exhausting. I willingly yielded my body into the comfort of the mattress.

11
Confined

It wasn't long before the news of my homecoming spread through the congregation. The phone again resumed its tireless ringing. Too weak to handle anything extra, including conversation, Phil protectively screened the calls.

This was one of those times when I was reminded that we were partially owned by many loving, concerned people. News of everyone's prayers trickled in. Concern and offers of help were abundant. Immediately a list was started for our meals. Cheryl organized the gigantic task of correlating food and getting interested women to come in twice a week to do the cleaning. I'd long since lost my pride about accepting help. In the beginning it was hard to receive, but no more.

Tensions melted away as I relaxed in this outpouring of love. I knew my family's physical needs would be met. It was apparent I would need help twenty-four hours a day and the question "What will I do during all the hours Phil is at work?" kept surfacing in my mind.

I longed to call my Mom and ask her to come help since she was only two hours away, yet I was hesitant to ask such a demanding favor. I knew she was free during the week. My father worked in construction and his jobs lately were all out of town. He was home only on the weekends but I was afraid she wouldn't be up to it healthwise. I feared our three rambunctious children would do her in.

As the day wore on, I slept fitfully. In my waking moments, I wrestled up the courage to give Mom a call. Previously I had told her of the church family's care for us and assured her all was well. Now, I desperately needed her for my emotional health. I concluded, "There's a time when only a Mom can fit the bill!" Grasping for the brown phone, I dialed the familiar number with trembling fingers.

After minutes of chit chat and beating around the bush I shyly asked, "Mom, do you think it would be possible for you to come over? I need you."

I sensed excitement in her voice. "Oh Honey, you know I'd love to! Your father's next job is in Bradenton, so maybe he could drop me off early Monday morning and then pick me up when he goes back on Fridays."

Her words brought relief and the prospects of having her close by for comfort excited me. We finished our conversation and I snuggled under the warm covers. "Just think I'll see Mom's green eyes on Monday."

Sleep was a welcome friend that weekend. Saturday seemed a blur with food, visits from friends, all sandwiched between rest. Sunday morning, I still felt drained. I knew it would take a while to regain my strength after the trauma of the weekend. The bleeding and labor cramping had pressed my muscles into a real workout and I was still sore from it all.

I could tell the adjustment from being active to bedridden would be a hard one for us. Our Sunday mornings were usually pretty hectic, but with me out of commission, all the responsibility rested on Phil's already overburdened shoulders. He awoke at his usual time of 4:30 a.m. and stumbled over to the church office to make final preparations and spend time in prayer for his morning message.

Returning home around seven, he prepared breakfast for the whole family. Things went fairly well until it was time for everyone to get dressed. David couldn't find his shoes, Holly had no idea what she should wear and Jonathan cried to get out of his messy high chair.

Oh, if only I could help I thought as I lay in bed catching glimpses of the rising bewilderment in Phil's lined face. For approximately an hour things grew from bad to worse until the kids somehow managed to get dressed and out the door. Jonathan still sniffled as he carried his blanket and sucked his thumb. His outfit was either too small or two big and his white blonde hair stuck out in all directions, but he was dressed.

"Whew!" Phil sighed as he hurried into the bedroom frantically jumping into the shower and then getting himself ready. They rushed out the door at 9:45 to dash into their respective Sunday School classes. Silence soothed me and I fell into a restless sleep plagued by dreams of dead babies.

A delicious Sunday meal was delivered and the aroma revived me. Settling back in his chair, Phil patted his full tummy, "M-m-m-m, that sure was good." But now all the breakfast and lunch dishes screamed for attention. "Time to get back to work," he stated as he tackled yet another task on his less than restful Sunday.

"I'll be glad when Mom gets here to help with some of this," I sighed. Tears dotted my pillowcase as I lay watching Phil doing work that I wished I could do.

"Lord, I know You have brought this series of events into our lives and you know what's best for us, but please give Phil extra strength. He works so hard for You and now to see him doing all my tasks on top of his.... Well, Lord, it breaks my heart. It's so hard for me to yield this part of me to You. Give us Your strength." My prayer uttered, I slipped into another nap with the dishes clinking a melodical lullaby.

Monday morning Mom called to let me know she would arrive sometime in the afternoon. Phil managed to get the kids ready and out the door in time to get to the bus stop.

Cheryl had arranged for several ladies to come in that day and do the cleaning and laundry. As the women arrived, I instructed them on what things needed done. They set about in a flurry.

My heart sank as I realized today was February 14, Valentine's Day. I hadn't even had a chance to pick up a present for Phil. Usually we went out to eat but there'd be no chance of that this year. I fought back feelings of self-pity. "C'mon, Sue, cheer up. This is God's will for you. It's for the best. Though things don't seem normal, this is how it's going to be for a while. You'll probably be in bed for only a week. It's not the end of the world. Get yourself together." My lecture finished, I decided to get up to take a very quick shower.

Stepping from the shower, I got myself fixed up so that when Phil came home for lunch I would at least look better. I fingered the ruffles on the collar of the white blouse with the little blue hearts. My thoughts rolled back to the day I bought it. "Well, I better wear this now. Who knows how long I'll be pregnant." I chose white slacks to complete the outfit.

Strength ebbed away easily every time I got up, so I forced myself to stay down. My two good friends, Cheryl and Marilyn, were there with others cleaning.

"Cheryl, would you come here? I never got a chance to get Phil a present. Do you think you could run to the store and get something for me to give him?" I questioned. She agreed.

The phone rang and Marilyn answered. "Sue, your

Sweetie's on the phone!" She grinned, handing me the phone and tiptoed out of the room. "Hi, Honey," his familiar voice cheerfully greeted. "Happy Valentine's Day!"

"Oh Hon, thank you." I gratefully sighed. "I was feeling so bad that I've messed up our romantic little dinner plans for tonight."

"That's why I called. What would you say if I went by and got us something special to eat for our lunch together? We can have our little celebration right there at home."

His thoughtfulness again overwhelmed me. "That would be great! But," I mischievously added, "what are we going to have?"

"Oh, how about if I surprise you?" he laughed.

"Well, that'll be just fine. But be sure and get something I like!"

"Marilyn," I called loudly from the room. "Could you come in here?" I excitedly shared our lunch plans with her and asked if she could help me fix up the room in a special way. She pulled the table over, put a pretty tablecloth on it and I instructed her as to what dishes to use. She brought me our colorful linen napkins. I folded them in a flower shape placing them on top of the blue and white dishes.

Then she brought my make-up over to the bed. I painstakingly applied it. All this activity tired me and I had to take frequent breaks to keep from getting too dizzy. Soon I looked like the Sue Phil was used to seeing. I knew he'd appreciate sitting across the table from someone who didn't look like a ghost.

Cheryl returned from the store. I stuck Phil's gift in a small bag next to the table. All the women planned on leaving around noon anyway so we would have some special moments of quiet. Jonathan was fed and put to bed and I heard Phil enter the front door.

He rustled around in the kitchen quite a while and soon made his way to my room. His little-boy grin widened as his hazel eyes twinkled. He placed a vase with a rose in it on the table. Next, he proudly displayed his carefully thought-out lunch.

Two fake crystal glasses were filled with my favorite shrimp and cocktail sauce.

"Oh Honey! I never expected this. Yum! It really looks good," I exclaimed as his smile widened even more.

Then he placed two plates on the table filled with my favorite Greek salad from a nearby restaurant.

"Wow! Oh, what a great idea, Phil! I can't wait to eat!"

He was obviously pleased with himself and I was thankful for this small, pleasant refuge from our struggles.

He closed the door and I gave him a loving, appreciative kiss. "Thanks so much for this, Hon. You've really made the day special in spite of our circumstances! I know it's not much but I had Cheryl pick this out for you." His eyes filled with surprise as he opened the small bottle of cologne.

"Oh," he grinned, "that was really sweet of you." He tenderly kissed me. "Hey, let's get on with our meal!" he laughed. We relished every bit of the scrumptious food and shared happy conversation. We were both painfully aware of how difficult our situation was, but we prayed we would cheerfully endure, buoyed by God's grace.

Mom arrived later in the afternoon and we all let her know how thrilled we were to have her help. When the kids got home from school, they were excited to have Nanny Gardner staying over. The den was now dubbed "Nanny's room." I still had doubts concerning Mom's health. I knew our household was much more active than hers was, living by herself during the week. I silently prayed God would give her patience and strength. Besides, I thought, it'll be only a week. I'll probably be up and around after that.

Jonathan shied away from her at first, but as the days wore on, they became real buddies and shared many giggles together.

12
Not My Will

Anticipation was another familiar passenger in our car as we drove to the doctor's office two days later. I was so pleased I still had the baby. I was sure the baby would be fine, and all would be well. We arrived at the office. Mom had never seen a sonogram before. "Lynne, do you think Mom could come into the room and see her future grandchild?" I asked.

"Sure," Lynne answered. We were pushing the small room to its occupational limits with Phil, Mom, Jessie (the ultrasound technician) and me. At first we were disappointed at our view of the baby, but Jessie pointed out the beating heart, baby's head, etc. I knew Mom was still having difficulty seeing it all. Satisfied she'd seen all that she wanted, we told her she could go back out and sit in the waiting room.

"Oh look!" I excitedly added, "both sacs are gone. Do you think the baby was harmed by all of this?"

"Wait a minute while I call Dr. Benson in," Lynne answered. Phil and I exchanged anxious looks. The mood had taken a somber tone and we didn't like the vibes we were getting.

Dr. Benson came in and viewed the screen. "How's our Bible baby?" she quizzed. I was amused at the name. Another doctor stepped in.

They pointed out that the amniotic fluid was much

95

lower and this explained why the baby looked so cramped. The doctors studied a couple of other views and then switched on the lights. They proceeded to explain their concerns.

"Sue, we think things are going to happen pretty soon. There must be a hole in the sac because the baby is really cramped from so little fluid. This means the baby could at times be squeezing the umbilical cord and choking out some of its air and nutrition. If it stays in a cramped position too long, some of the muscles could atrophy. The heartbeat was much slower today, which indicates the cord is being squeezed. When oxygen is cut off to the brain, it could impair your child's development".

Her words stabbed like knives, slicing away every spring of hope that had grown. I felt I was on a one way elevator, descending down, down, down, into a black hole.

Lynne completed the gloomy picture by adding, "You will need to stay in bed for the rest of this pregnancy. Only get up to go to the bathroom, because every time you get up you're leaking amniotic fluid. Continue to take your temperature every four hours because the risk of infection is high. If you start bleeding heavily again, come to the hospital immediately. There's a danger you could hemorrhage and that would be life-threatening to you."

Phil and I sat in stunned silence. Gathering our shocked emotions, we asked, "Well, does the baby have a chance? We know God can do miracles, but what's your medical opinion?"

"The baby's chances aren't real good. But there's always a hope that the hole torn in the baby's sac could heal. Beyond that," Lynne cryptically added, "only God knows."

Using Phil's arms for support, I made preparations

to leave the office and get in the car. He could set up my next week's appointment. Through tear-clouded eyes, I signaled to Mom in the waiting room and she helped me into the car. Soon Phil crawled in and set the car on its familiar course home. As we traveled, we tearfully explained to Mom all that we'd been told. We struggled as we let Mom know that if her grandchild made it, we faced the possibilities of a deformed or retarded child. Another tidal wave of emotion swept over me and I gasped for air.

Turning one familiar corner after another, I stared out the window and settled into silence.

I felt surges of God's grace ministering to me and I tearfully started singing, "It Is Well With My Soul." Phil regained some of his composure. As tears wet the black steering wheel, he joined me in our mournful songs of praise and victory. "Anywhere With Jesus" and "Count Your Blessings" ended our concert and I felt spiritually revived. God's strength lifted me to a platform one hundred stories high. I was on top of the world looking down.

I reached for Mom's tiny hand and gave it a vigorous squeeze. "I don't know what's going to happen, Mom, whether this baby will die or be deformed or what. But I know God has given us this trial in His love and I refuse to let my suffering be wasted. I am going to allow Him to use me all He wants and let Him get all the glory He possibly can."

Phil pulled up in front of the house and we sat in stillness, listening only to our breathing and sniffles. We were treasuring this sacred moment. We knew we were about to enter deep valleys and we felt we were treading on holy ground. It wasn't the road we had asked to travel but it was the road God had chosen. Our comfort was found in the assurance that He was right there with us, wrapping His arms around us and leading the way, one step at a time. Suddenly all our plans drastically changed. Mom knew she was going to be needed more than ever now, so she had to get back home to get her house in order. I overheard her slow, steady voice giving my Dad the not-so-happy news. I imagined Dad's clear, blue eyes clouding, his strong voice masking his tender emotions for his only daughter. How I longed to be a little girl again. Crawling on his lap, I would let my troubles go away! Yet I knew God was that kind of Father and as I shed my tears at His feet, He gave me His wise answer.

"Sue, you aren't that little girl anymore. I love you far too much to keep you in that childish state. Daughter, I must force you to grow up. These trials I'm allowing will work, for you, not against you. My child, I will not deliver you out of your circumstances, but I promise I'll give you comfort and peace in the midst of these storms. Hold on. My arms are wrapped around you. Learn from this time and through it all you'll come to know Me even more."

Peace flooded in as I sensed these unspoken words. I knew they were true and I would obey.

It was Thursday afternoon. Dad came and picked up Mom. I was relieved she would be back again on Monday, but I was apprehensive about what we'd do for extra help in the meantime. Phil assured me everything was under control.

That evening was once again a readjustment time. Phil hurriedly rushed around setting up the table for the kids and then preparing my lap tray. Women from the church continued supplying delicious meals. Having eaten, the dishes needed to be done and the kids' homework tended to. Jonathan showed his growing insecurity by demanding more attention. I tried to help, but he crawled on top of me and became a little too rough. The emotions of the previous day wore me down and I had no reserve.

Having to stay in bed was much harder now because I knew it could be a long time. I was growing more impatient and frustrated with my situation as I watched Phil in tired frenzy. By the time the kids were fed, washed and put in bed, Phil collapsed on the bed exhausted from his evening's work.

"Hon, I think this is going to be harder than we both imagined," I confessed as I brushed his brown hair from his forehead. He nodded and drifted into a heavy sleep.

Friday morning came quickly. The alarm pierced the early morning silence and I fumbled to turn it off. I automatically rose to get up and start breakfast when reality jerked me back down. Reluctantly, I shoved Phil's tired bones and he groaned.

Wrapping my arms around him and laying my head on his chest, I whispered, "Honey, I'm sorry, but it's time to get up. You need to get the kids' breakfast."

He struggled to unlock himself from his comfortable position as he groaned again. I hugged him as hot tears fell on his chest. "Honey, I'm so depressed. I wish I could get up and do things. It was so much easier when I thought I'd be in bed only a short while. Would you pray right now?" I tearfully pleaded.

He wrapped his arms around mine and petitioned God for strength, wisdom and patience for both of us. When he finished I felt a little better, yet a sense of dread and gloom hung over me.

Somehow Phil managed to get the entire family fed and the kids out the door in time to catch the bus. My friend, Cheryl, was going to come over and stay with me while Phil was gone, so he headed off to work.

I lay in bed trying to shake my feelings of self-pity. I tried to distract my thoughts by having my devotions and then reading the paper. Nothing worked. I still felt a dark cloud hovering over me. I knew it was time to reckon with my feelings.

A battle was raging inside me and I knew it. Once again I was fighting, struggling against God's will. All I could think of was months of lying on my back. Staying in this bedroom day afer day with nothing to do.

"What about my muscles?" I thought. I pictured my body turning into a round ball of flab. "If I don't get any exercise, I'll look terrible! I don't want to get fat and flabby!"

This was the crux of the whole matter, my pride. Keeping in shape had been such a way of life. I never realized pride had crept in. All my insecurities spewed from my mind.

"But Lord, I'll be repulsive if I get fat. No one will want to be around me. I'm Your ambassador and I want You to be proud of me," was my weak argument, but I knew it was futile. His Holy Spirit was convicting me and I knew I had to yield my will once again.

I grasped for my Bible and reviewed some comforting verses in Psalms. Everywhere I looked I gained assurance that God's purposes were better than mine. He wanted me to yield this area of my life along with all the others. He wanted nothing held back.

"All right, Lord," I confessed, "I see You have shown me an area of pride in my life. I know my value in Your sight. I don't have to gain my importance from my outward appearance. I want to be beautiful and godly from the inside. Do what You want, Lord. I will no longer struggle. I confess my pride in this area. Forgive me, Lord. I do love You and want Your best. This bed will not be a place of confinement for me. Any place in Your will offers much more freedom than lots of places outside of Your will. Help me to have patience, Lord. Help me to be brave and to be a blessing to others!"

The dark cloud lifted. I felt a sense of relief knowing

the Lord had won another victory. What changes He was bringing in my life! I reflected on the many works He had performed in me these few months. I was taken from being an active, jogging wife and mother to a place of real humilty. My activities as a mother had ceased. I could no longer go to church. Not only was jogging out of the picture, but I could do nothing. Yes, even my emotions were constantly changing. My self-confidence was gone. I never knew when I would break down and cry. Everything that was normal to me was gone. He took it all and replaced it with His peace. What a contentment in doing His will! I knew He could even choose to take my baby and yet I knew His way was best.

I was truly learning that the only thing in life that mattered was Jesus, loving Him and doing His will. He took my self-confidence and replaced it with Himself.

My pillow and nightgown were wet with tears of joy. I knew I was ready to face the day. I got up to take a quick shower and get my clothes on.

Yielding my will to this new "ministry" gave me great freedom and peace. The days didn't pass quite as slowly as they had before. Mom returned on Monday morning and all of us settled into what was to be normal. There were many adjustments for us all.

Mom worked feverishly trying to make a dent in the mountain of laundry that had accumulated. I'm sure her bones were aching.

Though I always felt we lived in somewhat of a fishbowl, things were even worse now. At times it was difficult to get used to our lack of privacy. We weighed the never-ending visits with mixed emotions. I was thrilled to see people since I could no longer get out. I felt I was able to minister to those who came and it gave me a feeling of usefulness and value. But talking involved many emotions. Some visitors, though well-intentioned, stayed too long and I would be left completely exhausted.

The only moments of privacy Phil and I had were late at night. After everyone else was in bed, conversation would flow but only for a few minutes as we both fell into exhausted sleep.

13
Acceptance

It was hard to believe only a week had gone by. Somehow this week had felt more like a month. I was twenty weeks along (five months) and I was encouraged the baby had survived this long.

I had another sonogram and the baby's amniotic fluid was even lower. The baby's heartbeat was strong and he seemed to be kicking harder and more often.

Everyone thought something would happen soon. They were tellng us to be prepared for a premie.

On the way home, Phil and I discussed the possibilities of having a premie. I conjured up hope, thinking my baby would make it if it could last just a few weeks longer.

"Honey, would you call the hospital when we get home so we can find out what they do with premies? I want to be prepared. I also want to know what is done if the baby dies. Do we have a funeral or what?"

His face reflected concern. "Are you sure you want me to do all that now?"

"Yes," I answered emphatically. "I want to be a little more prepared. From all the doctors told us today, I think something's going to happen soon and I don't want to make a lot of decisions rashly."

We called Bayfront Medical Center and they referred us to a woman who was in charge of premies. We told her of our situation and asked her about the chances of our baby's survival.

Our hearts sank as she kindly let us know that a twenty weeker had almost no chance medically. She went into a great amount of detail to explain why this was true. My hopes plummeted. If the baby lasted till twenty four or twenty six weeks, there was at least a slim chance of survival.

We asked about funeral details and she gave excellent suggestions for us to consider. Returning the phone to the receiver, Phil came in the bedroom where I had been listening and gave a heavy sigh.

Tears were already falling. My hopes were being dashed. I had to face the realities of the situation. Depression loomed over me. Each day seemed so long and fragile now.

"I don't see how this can go on much longer, Phil. Every time I get up, I feel like I'm killing the baby. I know I'm leaking fluid. I've tried so hard. There's nothing else, humanly, we can do. It's truly in the Lord's hands."

Lynne sensed my growing depression at my next visit. "Sue, why not have Phil put a lawn chair outside so you can lie down. The change of scenery will do you good."

Phil gladly dug up our orange and white striped chair and I made a tortoise-paced trip to find my seat. It seemed so strange being outside in the crisp air. It was refreshing to recline in the chair and drink in all the sights and sounds of our quiet little yard. Greedily I took in the bright blue of the sky and pure white clouds. Birds chirped busily as they flapped about searching for food in the grass. Our many oak trees still held greenish brown leaves, though many had already made their journey to the soil below. Pushing my face heavenward, I surveyed the blue sky with the oak branches providing stark contrast against the heaven's soft beauty. God's presence always seemed so real when I studied His realm. I longed to be free physically, floating as the clouds or flying as the birds.

"Oh Lord," I silently asked, "how long will I be tied down like this? I feel so bound." His heavens loomed huge and pure. I was awed at the greatness of a God who created all that.

"My heart cries out to You, Lord. I know You are big enough to handle all my problems. I feel so insignificant in comparison to these large heavens of Yours. I am awed that You are my God and that You do care about my feelings right now. Thank You for reminding me of Your greatness. I don't have the answers to all my questions, but I know You are in control and will give me Your answers in Your time." I smiled upward and imagined Him looking back with a corresponding smile.

Softly I whispered, "I love you, Lord," and gentle tears punctuated my statement. As I rose from my little altar and came inside, I decided I needed more of those quiet fellowships with my Lord. Instead of having my morning devotions inside, I would now go to my "outdoor chamber" and share sweet communion with my Father.

The hours clicked by and one day crept into another. Ever since our Wednesday visit to the doctor, I felt a sense of urgency about getting details worked out. I felt like a crystal glass ready to break. "I'm gonna stay completely flat at all times and only make absolutely necessary trips," I sternly thought. I began reading articles about premies. Sadly, the realization sunk in that having a premature infant would be no bed of roses. I handed these articles to Phil and my Mom. Their downcast looks and heavy sighs after reading the material told me they were contemplating the same things. If we thought we were going through life and death struggles now, just wait and see what would happen when we had a premie. Being born early meant a long hard fight for all concerned. "Oh God, I just don't know if I can handle that. But believe me, I want to try. Please let this baby live."

The more I thought of these things the more I felt pressured to talk to Phil about the possibility of a funeral. We jointly decided we would have a memorial service at the church, inviting all our friends and family.

We realized some people might think it silly to have such a large affair for a life not yet introduced, but we felt strongly about the value of this little life. This child was already loved and part of our family. If he died, we needed to give his birth/death all the meaning God intended. We knew we had to tell his story, for in doing so, we would be sharing him with others.

As far as the burial was concerned, I knew I wanted a small graveside service with only our family attending. My mind flashed back to the first time I went to the graveside of an infant. The young couple in our church who lost their daughter from Sudden Infant Death Syndrome had a moving graveside service. We were all still numb from the shock. Seeing the size of that delicate white casket jolted us all into reality and no one held back tears. If I had to look at my child's casket, I knew it would be extremely difficult and very personal. I would want to grieve in that moment with family and let us all shed tears together.

"Phil, if the baby dies, do you think you would be able to handle giving the memorial service and all?"

"Honey, I know God would give me the grace. I'd really want to do it myself," he affirmed.

I felt relief as we discussed our decisions. I knew it would be difficult to make choices in the throes of grief and the more things we talked over and decided ahead of time the better.

Friday, I gave Mom a hug as she left for the weekend. She looked tired and drained. The heaviness of the last few days was exhausting. I prayed she would get some rest.

Friends continued to call and come and go. More silence than words filled the air when I'd tell them of our recent decision. I felt they needed to be prepared for what might happen.

One woman refused to give up. "I'm claiming this baby for God!" she said confidently, "I just know everything's going to work out fine!"

"But the baby could die," I cautioned. "It's not that I don't have faith that God could do a miracle, but He's given me a peace that the miracle could be the baby's death and homegoing. We need to be able to accept whatever His will is."

"But Sue, I just feel like things will all work out. He's allowed the baby to live so far through many situations. I really think He's going to give you a healthy, happy baby," she insisted.

Her words brought no comfort, only frustration. I realized now how important it was to live by God's Word and not by feelings. I assured her I trusted in God and knew He could deliver this child if He wanted to, but I must also accept His will in the matter.

"How come God's told you the baby would be fine when He hasn't even shown me?" I asked. I shared with her that I knew whatever happened, we must all allow God's answer. Even Jesus prayed, "Not my will but Thine be done." The comfort I needed now was found in the promises of God's Word, I explained, and a friend can't offer comfort if they're not willing to accept God's decision. I think she got my point. I prayed that I hadn't offended her.

14
The Roller Coaster Plummets

February 26, Saturday, I had a fitfull night's sleep. I awoke off and on, feeling rather strange and having Braxton-Hicks contractions (early, minor contractions that prepare the body for serious labor). By morning, I felt more exhausted than when I went to bed. Slipping from underneath our covers to answer my "morning call," I was confronted with bright red blood.

"Oh no, not again." I called for Phil and awakened him from sleep.

"Honey, come here. Does this look bright red to you?" I shouted. He jumped out of bed and came to the bathroom. His eyes widened at the sight of the red blood. "You better call the doctor."

We had both been told the importance of checking for any change of color in the bleeding. It was stressed over and over again that I could hemorrhage, and we would need to respond quickly. Yet still, I hestitated to call. I was there only two weeks ago. I hated going back. It upset the kids so.

"Are you sure I should call the doctor, Phil? Maybe it's nothing."

"No, Hon. You remember what they said. If it turns to bright red, call."

Tearfully, I called the well-memorized number. I explained what happened and Lynne ordered, "Get down to the hospital right away."

I cried harder, "But do I have to? Are you sure it's something I have to go in there for?"

She empathized, "Sue, I know this isn't easy. I know you're tired, but I'm not only concerned about the baby. I'm concerned about you. If you hemorrage, you could die...bleed to death. Please come down."

"Okay," I glumly answered.

"And don't take time to get yourself prettied up. Come now!" she emphasized.

My appearance was the last thing on my mind. "Believe me, I don't feel like doing anything. I'll come soon."

Quickly I dialed Phil's Mom. At first all I could do was cry. "Mom, I'm bleeding again. They want me down at the hospital. Could you guys come over and watch the kids?"

"Sure, Sue. We'll be right over."

Next, I called my mother and told her where I'd be and asked her to pray for me.

"Oh, I'll pray, honey. I'll call some of my friends now. You sure you don't want me to come back over there?"

I assured her we had plenty of help for the time and we'd keep her posted.

Tears continued to flow as I gathered my things. Fortunately, I had left my bags packed. I had sensed that we might have to leave in a hurry again.

The kids began asking questions. Jonathan sensed we were leaving and started to cry. I longed to pick him up and comfort him, yet I knew the strain of lifting him could do even more damage. I stooped down and cradled him in a hug as my tears mingled with his. Holly's blue eyes filled with concern. She hugged me and said, "Oh, Mommy, I wish you didn't have to go."

"I know, Honey. I do too, but the doctor says I have to come."

"Did your bubble break?" David nervously interrupted.

"No, Honey. I'm bleeding again."

"Do you think you'll have the baby?" he asked.

"Well, maybe," I answered, "but if I do, the baby might die. He's still too small to survive. God would have to do a miracle for him to live."

"Oh," he answered, not fully understanding the magnitude of what I said.

Phil's parents arrived and his mother rushed into our bedroom.

"Oh, Mom, I don't want to go to the hospital again! I'm so tired! I've tried so hard...", I ended in a mass of sobs.

She patted me affectionately. "I know, Sue. But you must go. We're concerned about you. You could hemorrhage or something."

"I know," I answered as I wiped the tears from my face and gained some composure.

Phil had frantically thrown all our things together. He went outside to pull the car around to the front so I'd have fewer steps to walk. When he beeped, I slowly made my way to the door, kissed the kids goodbye and crawled into the car with the sound of Jonathan's cry ringing in my ears. "Oh Lord, this is so hard on all of us. Please comfort the kids," I prayed.

I felt we'd worn a rut in the road leading to and from the hospital. As we sped to our familiar destination, an unwanted pang crept through my back and stomach. "Oh no!" I thought. "Contractions!" I tried not to let them come, but sheer will power couldn't hold my body back. The contractions were coming with increasing regularity.

The nurses wheeled me into the all-too-familiar check-in room for labor and delivery. Lynne arrived and began her work. As she checked me, I didn't want to tell her I was having contractions, but soon the secret was discovered. My belly grew tight and came to a high mountain-like lump in the middle. "When did the contractions start, Sue?" Lynne inquired.

Shakily, I replied, "On the way down here." Glancing toward the floor, I added, "They seem to be coming harder and more often."

The laugh lines were gone from Lynne's face. She turned to a nurse. "Let's put her into a room. She's going to be here a while." She continued to briskly order all sorts of tests while they wheeled me out of the room.

Phil stayed with me every minute. I clung to every ounce of strength he could silently give. His presence helped keep me under control. As the contractions continued to come, what little hope we had in reserve was slowly being sucked away. Nurses scurried in and administered vistrol and demerol to stop the contractions.

While more blood work was being done, they strapped the fetal monitor on. Lynne came to my bedside and gently squeezed my hand. She was watching the monitor.

I didn't want to, but I forced the question from my lips that everyone knew I would ask, "How's the baby doing?"

"Well," Lynne hesitated, "...it looks like the baby's in some distress. With each contraction you have, the baby's heartbeat is slowing too much." She explained what the normal range for the heartbeat was, yet the fetal monitor's flashing red digital numbers revealed far from satisfactory readings.

My eyes stayed riveted to the monitor. I tried to will those numbers to change, yet I knew it was to no avail. The red numbers grew fuzzy and faded into one luminous color as tears obscured my vision. My hopes collapsed, I turned my head and stared at the hospital's green walls. I just wanted out of the whole situation.

Lynne read my thoughts. She clicked off the machine and loosened the tummy belt. "I don't think we need to watch the baby die," she almost angrily stated. I sensed her frustation and sorrow. I knew she had also come to the same conclusion as I. My baby was going to be born today, born to die.

All the gloomy statements about a twenty-week-old's chance for survival rang in my ears. "They're just too little...no needles small enough for those tiny veins..eyes not open yet...." I was ready for everything to be over with.

I surveyed Phil next to my bed. Our hands clasped, his head down. He looked so tired, so burdened. His luminous smile was gone. Lynne felt our need to be alone. She slipped out of the room as Phil came to my left side and pulled down the silver bed rails. The upper half of his body crumpled and he tenderly laid his head on my chest. His release had come. He was willing to let go now and he heaved in mournful sobs. All the hope we both had felt was draining out with each wretching tear.

My heart ached to see him so sad, yet I had no more tears to give. I was just so tired. Numbness obscured my emotions.

"Oh Honey," he sobbed, "I was just sure this baby was going to make it, and now...now, I know we'll never hear this baby cry. Oh, I wanted this baby so bad...." His voice was again drowned in oceans of tears.

I stroked his brown hair. I, too, had already come to this point of resignation and now I just wanted things to get over with quickly.

I had been having contractions since 9:15 a.m. Now, I welcomed each one, hoping this would all soon end. It was noon and I noticed the contractions starting to back off. Was the demerol and vistrol beginning to work? What irony! Now that I wanted the contractions to come, they were slacking off! "Oh Lord!" I sighed, "is this a cruel joke? Can't you just take me out of this whole mess? Please don't taunt me with hope again!"

Phil sensed a change. "Have your contractions backed off?"

I wished he hadn't asked. I didn't want to answer. "Well," I stumbled, "I...I think they have."

It was 2:15 p.m. and seemingly all contractions had stopped. Lynne walked in and hooked up the monitor. Miraculously, the digital numbers were in the normal fetal heartbeat range. We all froze in silence, staring at the continuing numbers in disbelief. The rhythmic thump, thump, thump of the baby's heartbeat scraped together any fragment of hope and dished it into my brain.

Silently, I waged a war. "No!" I said, "I don't want to hope again. I'm tired! I want to push you away, Hope. Don't come in here again! It hurts too much." Yet the steady thumping broke through my mental frontline and plainly won the war. The seed of hope was again sown in the soil of my reluctant heart.

Phil's childlike grin came back. "Lynne," he excitedly questioned, "you mean the baby's still alive and well? Sue's contractions have stopped. That's a good sign, isn't it?"

Lynne shrugged her shoulders. "I just don't know, Phil, I mean, maybe her contractions will start up again. I just don't know. This is all so crazy. I thought for sure you were losing the baby this time. I never would've believed it. I'll say it again—only God knows!"

She gave me a hesitant hug. "Are you doing okay?"

"Yeah," I softly answered, "I guess so. When can I go home?"

With disbelief still clinging to her words, Lynne replied, "Well, I guess if everything is still stable in the morning, you may go home then."

I could hardly believe it. Here it was, Saturday afternoon, and I had been sure by Sunday we would be announcing our baby's death in church. So many incredible things were happening. If I wasn't so tired, I would've cheered. Phil and I again cemented our hope in a hug.

Sunday morning. My eyelids were about the only part of my whole body that didn't ache, though they were red and swollen from the crying of the day before. I still had that sick feeling in the pit of my stomach like when you've been awakened from a bad dream. Instantly, I slid my hand down to my tummy, just to check and make sure the baby was still there. The ever-familiar kicks were now more precious than ever.

"Well, baby, it's truly a miracle that you're still here and alive. You sure are a fighter," I silently thought.

Both Lynne and the doctors let me know that we weren't out of the woods yet. I was carefully informed to take my temperature every four hours to make sure there was no infection. Lying still and flat was more imperative now since the risk of infection and further rupture of the membranes was easier. I knew under normal conditions I probably would've been told to stay in the hospital, but I think Lynne had assured all concerned that I would be a good girl.

Phil had gone home under my urging the night before so he could get a decent night's sleep. His contagious grin was first to appear around the corner. He looked so handsome in his deep brown suit. I knew he was cutting into his Sunday morning preparation time to come and get me, but he insisted on coming before Sunday School. There were no traces of Saturday's strain on his ruddy complexion and his blue-green eyes danced as he said, "Well, I hear I get to take my wife and baby home today."

I managed a weak smile. Thoughts of home and familiar surroundings pricked a little life into my weary muscles. As I lay in bed, I gingerly put on my maternity clothes. Soon, I was in a wheelchair and going out the doors. We slipped into the Honda and headed for home.

15
The Temperature

It took every ounce of my reserve energy just to get out of the car and maneuver my way into the bedroom. My cozy bed welcomed me again and I snuggled under the covers with pleasure. Once settled in, Phil sat down softly on the edge of the bed and affectionately stroked my hair and face.

"Mom and Dad will bring the kids here after church. Are you sure you'll be all right by yourself?"

I promised I'd call if I needed any help. "Right now, I'm just so tired. All I want to do is sleep, Honey. You go on to church...I'll pray your sermon goes well."

Phil gave me a gentle kiss and slipped out the door. Silence enveloped me and beckoned me into a dreamy world of rest. Without hesitation, I yielded and felt soothed by the sleep.

The normal family activity awakened me hours later. Holly, David, and Jonathan smothered me with hugs and kisses. We were all thrilled my hospital stay hadn't been a long one.

As the day progressed, I dutifully took my temperature and heaved a sigh of relief at each normal reading.

Phil scurried around getting the kids and himself ready for Sunday evening church. It was 5 p.m. and time for another temperature check. I stuck the thermometer in my mouth and three minutes later, nonchalantly, searched for the familiar 98.6 degree reading. My eyes landed on the mercury which had risen to 99 degrees. Fear gripped me.

"Maybe I made a mistake," I thought. "I'll take it again." This time it read 99.2. Phil stopped his preparations to glance over at me. He read my look of concern.

"It's normal, isn't it?"

I hated to confess the truth, especially just before the evening service. I didn't want to upset him. "Well...," I hestitated, "I'm a little worried. It's 99.2." Reassuringly, I added, "But maybe it's just a mistake. I'll check again at 5:30."

Satisfied temporarily with my answer he went back to his work. At 5:30 on the dot, Phil brought me the thermometer and stuck it under my tongue. Waiting an eternal four minutes, he pulled it from my mouth.

"99.8. Sue, I want you to call Lynne right now. You know what they said about the risk of infection."

Lynne confirmed our fears. "If your temp goes to l00.4 you need to go to the hospital immediately. Your risk of infection is so high. If we wait too long, we could lose you. This is nothing to mess around with."

I pushed out my unwanted questions, "Would this mean I'd lose the baby?"

"We'd have to take the baby if you had an infection, because the baby wouldn't survive. If we waited too long, we'd lose you too."

My heart pounded. Thoughts were scrambling inside my flushed head. "Oh Lord, please don't let it end this way!"

"Okay, Lynne," I understand. "I'll keep careful watch and do what you say if the fever goes higher."

Phil was reluctant to go to church, but I knew I could always call if something were to happen quickly.

Our house was only a hundred yards from the church. He gave me a strong hug and left, apprehension shading his brow.

Moments later, the front door opened and our two "adopted" daughters walked in. Debbie and Mary had been taken into our hearts when they were in their teens. We had talked, loved and cried through numerous good and bad times together. They affectionately referred to us as Mom and Dad.

As they entered the bedroom, I guessed Phil had sent them over by the worried looks on their faces. I explained the situation to them. They tearfully hugged me and offered their support. Determined to stay and care for me during Phil's absence, they joined me in a silent vigil.

I was so confused. Adamantly opposed to abortion, I didn't know if I should let them take the baby. I desperately wanted to talk to someone who had the medical knowledge I needed who was also a commited Christian. Immediately, I thought of my previous gynecologist, Dr. Ruth Perry. I asked Deb and Mary to pray with me before I called her. Tears dampened the comforter as we fervently prayed for God's wisdom.

Dr. Perry was already aware of some of my difficulties, so I filled her in on the latest details. She knew and shared my convictions about abortion, so she could tell what I was thinking. "You would lose the baby anyway if you developed an infection, Sue. Something will definitely need to be done soon if you are to remain healthy."

Confusion still plagued me. I felt I'd just have to leave all this in God's hands, because I was too frail to make any decisions at the moment.

"Sue, I'll pray your fever comes down. In fact, let's pray right now."

Over the phone, Ruth led in a beautiful prayer that

brought peace and comfort. "You call me if anything else happens," she said.

At five minutes till seven, Phil called to get a last minute check on my temperature before he went into the service. It remained at 99.8. The hour passed slowly. At 8 p.m. Phil rushed home and anxiously asked what my temperature was.

"It's 99.7," I answered, afraid to feel any relief yet. Every fifteen minutes I checked and it steadily descended until at 9 p.m. it reached the normal reading. Our tensions released into a pool of tears. Debbie and Mary finally consented to go home when we promised to call them if anything else happened.

That evening, as I rested my head on my favorite spot, Phil's chest, I listened to his rhythmic breathing. Silently, I thanked God for saving our baby one more time.

The following days were filled with sleep and rest. Every evening, I noticed Braxton-Hicks contractions come and go. I knew in my heart this child wasn't going to wait much longer.

My mother continued to come during the week and help with the kids. She tried to hide her apprehension, but her green eyes told another story. I tried to keep things light, but that evening I started having contractions again. We were alone while the rest of the crew was at prayer meeting. An eerie feeling that something else was about to happen crept over me. I had felt light-headed and weak all day. My bleeding had increased and the contractions were a little stronger. "Why don't you go to bed now, Mom? I'm okay. You get your rest."

"Are you sure, Hon? I don't mind staying up."

"No really, I'll be fine. I'll just read a while." Satisfied, she went to bed.

Phil and the kids burst through the door,

interrupting my silence. Hurriedly Phil got them in bed and walked into the bedroom. Sensing my tension he quizzed, "Are you okay, Honey? You look kind of pale."

"I...I don't know how to explain it, Hon, but I sense something's going to happen tonight. Maybe I've gotten so good at reading my body that I can tell when something's wrong."

"Well, I guess all we can do is wait," Phil added. "We should be getting better at this. Seems like that's all we do anymore—wait."

At 9:30 another rushing surge came. Quickly I bolted to the bathroom. A strange sensation settled in along with cramping. I checked in the toilet bowl to see how heavy the bleeding was. A small dark object settled to the bottom. It was about the size of a fifty-cent piece.

Tingling pricked my fingers. My heart stopped. With horror, I groped for the sterile cup Lynne gave me just in case something like this would happen. I forced myself to catch the tissue, fearing I'd see an arm or a leg. My heart beat wildly as blood pumped through my veins at what seemed a hundred-mile-an-hour pace. Was this part of the baby? What awful thing was happening? I peered at the lump in the cup. It resembled liver and was grayish red.

Phil grew concerned as he waited for me to return from a supposedly quick bathroom trip. Opening the door, I excitedly thrust the cup into his face, "What do you think this is?"

His eyes widened and his face contorted in a grimace. We both stared in disbelief. "I...I don't know," he answered in bewilderment.

"I don't either. It scares me to death, though. Do you think it's the baby? I better call Lynne."

I quickly dialed her number. My mind did an instant replay. Stress pushed me into giddiness. Suddenly the whole situation seemed strangely funny. Lynne waited apprehensively as I giggled in between sentences. I told her every detail of this latest weird event.

"Well now, Sue. Try and control yourself. You say you passed some tissue. What exactly does it look like?"

I had an uncontrollable urge to laugh. Stifling tears and laughter I explained, "Well, it's...it's red and well...well, it looks like a (suppressed laughter) chicken liver! But I know one thing. I know it's not that!" Laughter exploded on both ends of the phone.

As I wiped tears from my face, I heard Lynne say, "Well, Sue, I knew you were weird, but I know you're not that weird!"

We continued in our tension-releasing laughter for a few more minutes. Lynne explained, "It's probably just a piece of old blood. Bring it into the office for a thorough check tomorrow...and Sue, try and get some rest."

The following day, I was checked. Everything remained the same. The lab report from the tissue came back reading, "fragments of degenerating debris." Lynne continued to tease, "How's your chicken liver today, Sue? What other weird surprises do you have to liven up my week?"

Laughter did me a lot of good. It had been a long time. Relief from the lab report helped me go home in peace. Life proceeded again.

Jonathan came down with some kind of flu and I longed to hold and rock him. I wanted to be a normal mother again, not tied to a bed. He was sick all Tuesday evening with diarrhea, vomiting and a 104 degree temperature. Phil tended to him most of the night, but after seeing his exhaustion, I told him I'd take over a little while. Though I knew it was taking a risk, I got up and walked back to Jonathan's room. I lay down next to him, put a cool cloth on his head and prayed with him. I drank in the chance to be his mommy again. His fever eased and the next morning he was recovering quickly.

16
A Price I Had To Pay

Tuesday, March 8, I was very weary and couldn't do much except rest all day. Guilt shrouded me in a dark cloud. What if I lost the baby simply because I got up the night before and tended to my sick child? I knew I had to share these fears with Phil. During all these struggles our marriage had been tremendously strengthened. Our oneness was so special and growing. We had truly become part of one another, drawing strength from each other. I knew I needed a good transfusion of his strength.

Phil slowly tore little holes into my shroud of guilt. His gentle reminders of God's faithfulness and love soothed me. "Honey, God is much bigger than our mistakes. His sovereignty is a big measuring stick. He knows what He's doing, even if we don't. Trust Him with your fears."

My love for Phil grew in these heart-to-heart times. He was so gentle and humble and could explain God's truths so clearly. He drew me closer to the Lord because I saw His presence in Phil's life. I desired that kind of relationship too. His unselfishness and tenderness touched me. The guilty shroud was gone. I once again placed my life and my child into God's hands.

Light contractions began about 4:30 p.m. I played no mental games this time. It seemed my child's birth was soon to come. I knew a couple of weeks would change the baby's survival rate for the better, but sheer will power couldn't prevent labor. Quietly and calmly I informed, "Phil, Mom, contractions have started." No games or laughter. Serious business was underway.

As we apprehensively waited, the contractions grew stronger. By 10 p.m., they were about three to five minutes apart and much more intense. I knew a phone call to Lynne would mean another trip to the hospital, but I was ready.

Our blue luggage lay in its same position from our previous visit. There was no frantic rush or panic this time. We deliberately set about our last minute tasks. Phil woke Mom. She sat on the couch silent and somber. After dressing, I made my way to each of my sleeping children's beds. They never felt the wet tears I dripped beside each pillow. They were off in a slumber world of peace and happy things. I didn't want to place dying babies in those dreams. Quietly, I planted kisses on each blonde head and pink cheek. It seemed I would be gone a million years and I knew I would not return with a chubby-cheeked baby brother or sister. My hope was again at an all time low and leaving the house was more difficult than it had ever been.

As we sped toward the hospital, an eerie calm settled over my spirit. God had evidently given His hypodermic of grace. Phil glanced over at me nervously. I was breathing deeply, trying to relax with each intensifying contraction. Knowing all my physical struggles would be over after this night, a strange sense of relief came over me.

Lynne wasn't on call, so Ann's somber face met us in the labor room. She checked me and confirmed I was dilated two centimeters.

"I can feel the baby's head," she stated, swiftly removing the surgical gloves with a snap.

Heaving a sigh, I asked, "Well, what do we do now?"

"We have several options, Sue...," her voice seemed to fade out as I visualized my dying baby in my weary arms.

Phil and I wanted to give one last chance to our precious little one. There was a possibility of stopping my labor if they administered magnesium sulphate. We decided to give it a try.

My legs began an uncontrollable shaking. Fear gripped me as the green-walled hallway sped by. The clank of metal instruments and opened bottles heightened the shaking of my legs. I felt helpless on that cold lonely bed. Phil gripped my hand as our eyes followed swiftly moving nurses. Ann's smile was absent. She was serious and business-like.

"Sue, we're going to crank the foot of the bed up to help gravity a little. We want to try and keep that baby inside. We're also going to have to catheterize you, because we have to keep a close check on your kidneys. It will take me ten minutes to push the magnesium sufphate into your bloodstream, because it has to be done slowly. You may feel a burning sensation and possibly some nausea."

The piercing of the catheter burned. Emotions scrambled. Fear gripped me tightly. I felt my air being choked out. The stab of the IV needle into my right hand surged pain up my arm. The end of the bed raised toward the ceiling and blood rushed to my head. My body unwillingly slid toward the head of the bed. I gripped the bedrails in a futile attempt to stop the process. I wanted to yell "Stop!" but panic silenced the words. Helplessness seized me. "What are they doing? What have I done? Oh, God, why do I have to go through this?"

I searched Phil's blue eyes for strength, too petrified to speak. I felt violated, humiliated, so many confusing emotions. As a snake slithers from its skin, I wanted to shed this body of mine and leave that room. Phil sensed my fragile state and his grip squeezed tighter. Contractions grew stronger. Trying to relax was impossible.

Ann appeared at my right side with a large needle. Slowly, she eased it into the IV. I felt an icy hot stream rush into my arms and into my veins.

"Now, Sue, you may feel warm, but don't worry. Just relax and let the medicine do its work."

I felt as if I were standing on my head and tried pulling up to avoid bashing the headboard. Suddenly, fire coarsed through my veins. I gasped for air. Surely my blood wasn't boiling, but it felt like hot lava had invaded my veins. Air rushed from my lungs to be replaced by fire.

Violently I jerked my head to the left and with a wide-eyed look of panic squeezed Phil's hand till my knuckles turned white. "Oh Honey, oh Honey. I'm so scared! I'm so hot. This is awful. What's happening? I'm on fire!" I thrust my face to the ceiling. "Oh, God! Oh God! I'm scared. Help me! Help me!" The fire softened my voice to a wilted whisper.

Beads of sweat emerged on my forehead. I flailed back to the right. Ann's calm eyes studied me as she continued the torturous IV push. Empathy oozed from her brows, but the relentless push went on. "Only a few more minutes, Sue," she added apologetically.

Simultaneous emotions I never knew I could feel surged through me. Fear, panic, anger, helplessness, sorrow were crowded together in my shaking body. Panting didn't put out the fire. It only dried my already parched lips. Nausea rushed in. My panic heightened. My eyes pleaded silently with Phil for rescue, but he was only a helpless spectator. I wretched uncontrollably. Death seemed close at hand. In between heaving, frail whispers of prayer crept from my cracked lips. "Oh Lord!" I knew the spirit interpreted those words into the long eloquent prayers I had no strength to give.

Ann's relentless push finally ceased. The fire cooled a little but still smoldered in my veins. The nausea subsided. I searched for the Lord's face in that white ceiling. "You know I'm going through this agony because I want to obey You. It would've been easier for me to let them take this little life, but You knew I couldn't do it. I love You, Lord. Thank You for being here with me. Thank You for holding my hand. Thank You for giving me the strength to really live my convictions. It's not just words anymore. You know I've proved in my life I don't believe in abortion even if this is the hard way out. You've given me the strength to go through this." My unspoken prayer calmed me and dulled the ache in my head and body.

With little strength to talk, I tried to push words of reassurance to Phil. "Thank you, Honey. Your support really helps." His anguish was obvious.

The intense effect of the medicine lessened. I tried in vain to sleep. The continual headstand position kept me from it. Contractions still came but eased in intensity. Baby continued to give reassuring kicks.

By 4:30 a.m. on Wednesday, March 9, the contractions subsided. That morning, they wheeled me down for another sonogram and it was confirmed. This baby was ready to be born. All the amniotic fluid was gone and the baby's head was down. Tearfully, Phil and I agreed the battle was over. A numbness overtook me as they discontinued the medication and cranked my bed into a flat position. Now, it was time to wait and let God put things into action.

Thoughts flooded my mind, but Ann entered and interrupted them. "I know this was an awfully hard decision for you to make, but I think you did the right thing."

She reached for my hand then slid down to give me a hug. Tears spilled down my cheeks as I nodded in agreement. She added, "You know last night I went home and told my husband all about you and Phil. I told him you guys were the kind that give faith a good name."

God's boldness and sustaining grace mustered a reply from my lips. "Well, you know, Ann, faith is what sustains us. A lot of people say they have faith until something bad happens. Then, everything is forgotten. But I strongly believe that a Christian can have bad things happen to them. It's a testing of our faith. When I was sixteen, I put my faith in Jesus Christ as my Savior. Someone told me that Christ died in my place for all my sin. All I needed to do was pray and ask Jesus Christ to save me and forgive me for all I'd done wrong. When I did that, I became His child. I know He allows these 'bad' things to happen because He loves me. That doesn't mean I don't hurt. It doesn't mean I understand it all. If I did, I wouldn't need God. He's allowing Phil and me to go through this for many reasons and He is the one who gives us strength to go on. Faith in other people can fail you, but faith in Jesus Christ won't. I have to give Him all the credit. He's always there."

She soaked in every word and nodded in agreement as she gave me a final squeeze. "I'll check in on you later."

My final waiting for this baby had begun. Minutes crept by as Phil and I silently walked through the last hours of this pregnancy. My fear and apprehensions grew as time passed with no contractions. Baby didn't kick as often, but when I felt the movement, I quietly wept. It was the realization these were probably his last kicks. Grief over this little fighter was building like a gathering storm. I knew we were experiencing the eye of this hurricane, soon to be followed by throes of labor that would produce a child dead or dying.

Into this heavy atmosphere an attractive brown-haired woman entered. "Hi! I'm Cathy. I'm here to help you in any way I can. I deal with parents of premies and stillborns." At first, it was hard for me to pull myself out of the self-imposed, dulling fog. I didn't want to delve into this horrible new world of dying babies. Yet I knew I must face it. My fears about the whole situation overtook me and I fired out many questions. A stillborn baby had only been viewed in my nightmares, so I was afraid the baby would look grotesque or malformed. I wanted to know if my labor would be long and hard. Would it be painful? What did the hospital do with dead babies? If the baby was breathing, wouldn't there be some chance for survival?

Her soft-spoken manner calmed me. Understanding surrounded her answers. She lovingly and slowly explained how big our baby would be and how normal it would probably appear. We would have to make last minute decisions about baby's care depending on its condition. She assured us they would do everything to make the child warm and comfortable. Since this baby was only a twenty-three-weeker, they wouldn't be able to do much. They didn't even have tubes and needles small enough for a child that size. My hopes for something miraculous to happen were fading. I was beginning to realize that medical science at this point in time hadn't advanced far enough to help my baby. Tears again wet my pillow.

She encouraged us to hold, touch and stroke the baby all we wanted, instructing, "After all, it will be your child and you may have only a short time to get to know him before you have to say goodbye. We'll have a Polaroid camera here so you can take pictures. You can even arrange to let your family and children see the child if that's what you really want. We'll try to help you any way we can." With that she squeezed my hand and reminded me to call her if I needed her help again.

Her kind counsel encouraged me. I felt a small surge of strength enter to help me through the next difficult moments.

Phil's stomach was growling. The sound signaled that lunch time was near. All morning had passed with no contractions, so I was sure it would be a while before anything happened.

"Honey, why don't you go down and get something to eat? I'm sure I'll be all right. Besides, you'll need your strength for today."

"Are you sure you will be all right?" he questioned.

"Yes. Maybe I need a few minutes alone anyway, to pray and think."

He consented and left, promising not to be gone long. Five minutes after he left, I felt a twinge in my stomach. I waited. Maybe I was just imagining things. I took mental note of the time. Ten minutes later, I felt another squeeze-twinge. I prayed I wouldn't get another. The time was 12:30 p.m. and I knew the twinges had formed into contractions. My labor had begun. Tears spilled down my cheeks as my legs began shaking. I knew what was about to happen. The eye of the storm had passed. Fear, panic and sadness overwhelmed me.

Just then, my Mom's face popped into view. She was accompanied by my lovely blonde-haired friend, Cheryl. They seized me in a wonderful three-some hug. Tears smeared our faces as we all nervously chuckled.

"My contractions have started again. It won't be long now."

My statement was met with more hugs and unashamed tears. "Oh Mom, soon it will be over. I don't want the baby to die, but I'm so tired. I believe with all my heart that I've given this baby every possible chance. I guess it's just not God's will." I buried my head in her arms. She kissed my face and uttered a tender prayer for me. "Dear Lord, please be with my frightened daughter. Give her Your strength to get her through this difficult time. We love you, Amen."

Phil rushed in and guessed what was happening. "Have you called the nurses and told them, Hon?"

"No, you need to do that. I think Lynne wants to know so she can be here."

Only minutes passed until the solemnity was broken by nurses bustling about clanking instruments and readying me. Cheryl gave me a final hug and tore herself from the room so she could go to the labor waiting lobby. Mom spoke up.

"If it's all right with you, Hon, I'd like to stay and see my grandchild born. I talked with Lynne and she said I could." Though surprised, I was relieved and welcomed her to stay. The violent leg shaking worsened. Lynne entered, and again, her presence calmed me. Efficiently and painlessly she inserted the IV tubes.

"We're going to give you some Pitosin so we can speed things up a little, Sue." Sensing my fear and unasked questions, she added, "I'm also giving you some Demerol to help you relax." Her quiet confidence stilled me. The medicine began to calm the shaking and relieve my panicky feeling.

I moved into a world of hazy calm, intermittently mixed with suppressed fear. The intensity of the contractions grew and so did the pain. Though I tried to relax even the hazy Demerol sleep couldn't remove the present realities from my mind. Too weak to really cry, my eyes poured forth a steady small drip.

Phil's somber face kept reappearing. I could sense his touch. Mom lightly stroked my arms, forehead and hair. She whispered in my ear, "You know, Honey, I want you to know I've never been more proud of you than I am in this moment. You're not my little girl anymore. You've grown into a lovely strong woman. I love you."

I longed to affirm my love for her in return but another contraction seized me. I choked back the reply.

Lynne checked me and said, "Sue, it won't be long now. With these next contractions, I want you to push."

Though everyone seemed rather hurried, I jerked into low gear. The world around me seemed to creep as if in slow motion. I focused in on pushing. Everything else was blocked out. An engulfing final push seized me and I knew our baby was born.

"What is it?" I asked.

"It's a boy!"

Lynne wrapped him in a blanket and held out the tiniest of humanity I'd ever seen. She laid him on my chest. The chaos and horror I assumed would accompany this moment were absent. An all-pervading stillness and peace flooded me. I smiled as I viewed my tiny son. "Michael Tim Engelman...hello," I whispered.

Awestruck by his completeness, I examined each part of his fragile body. I could hold him in my one hand. Each little finger and toe, even minute toenails were there. His feet were half the size of my thumb and his head was about the size of a small orange. There were no frantic cries or horror-stricken faces. One look at him and we all knew the miraculous beauty we beheld could survive only minutes.

"Is he alive?" I incredulously asked.

"Yes, his heart's beating but he's not really breathing." Lynne answered. His skin looked brown and I asked her why.

"He must have suffered some respiratory damage during your last labor. Also his skin is very transparent because there's no fat underneath it yet."

I had no doubts about his certain death. His toothpick-like arms and legs never kicked or moved. He felt limp. I longed to see his eyes, but just as I had been told, they were still sealed shut. I could see the family traits already firmly implanted. "Look at the cleft in his chin! See the Engelman nose?" I pointed to Phil. Glancing up, I could see Phil's tear-stained cheeks and sensed he longed to hold his son. Gingerly, I handed him over.

While Phil held the baby I tried to take it all in. I thought of the many babies this size who were aborted. How could it be? I knew that twenty-four weeks was the point in pregnancy when most abortion clinics shy away from performing abortions. Legally, a child can be aborted at any point in a woman's pregnancy if a good enough reason can be provided. Prior to the twenty-fourth week, no questions are asked. Here was a baby only twenty-three weeks along, and yet he was perfectly formed. I wondered if he could have survived had he never suffered the trauma of this troubled pregnancy. In a flash my already present revulsion at the thought of abortion was enhanced.

I searched for Lynne and realized she must have quietly completed her tasks and then slipped out. She knew Mom, Phil and I needed some time to ourselves.

17
Hello...and Goodbye

I heard a tiny, "Can I come in?" It was Cheryl's voice. Our eyes met, followed by the silence that only dear friends understand. We both knew there were no words for this moment, no way to put a name on it all.

Cheryl's shy smile broadened at seeing Michael. Phil handed him over to Mom where she sat on a chair in the corner of the room. Mom stared in wonder at his tiny features and shared the same sad, sweet smile we all displayed on our faces. I knew private thoughts were hard to verbalize. She merely looked up from her grandchild and loved me, eyeball to eyeball. Soon her moment was over and she handed him back to me. My body was beginning to remind me of all I had been through. Though my child never opened his mouth for that first wonderful cry, I still had given birth and overwhelming exhaustion seized me. I asked Cheryl if she wanted to hold the baby. Her blue eyes lit up as she answered, "Oh, I'd love to!" As she pulled back the blanket, she exclaimed, "Oh, he's so cute!"

I fell back into the comfort of the hospital white sheets. A nurse poked her head in the door and meekly asked for Michael. He needed to be weighed and checked over by a pediatrician just like all the other newborns. Each of these events comforted me, because it made me feel like he was a real human being and not something to be quickly forgotten or dismissed. He was a real baby. Cheryl surrenderd him into the nurse's arms.

Phil and Mom related all the vitals to Cheryl. My hard labor lasted only forty-five minutes and Michael was born at 2:49 p.m. It was obvious from the moment of birth that no pediatric team needed to be called. He was just too little and had suffered too much trauma.

Nurses whisked in and out, cleaning me, changing sheets. Not one looked me in the eye and said, "I'm sorry about your baby." I knew it was probably just their way of dealing with this sad event. I had told Lynne of my wishes for the family to come and see Michael and I assumed she was off somewhere arranging for it.

The familiar brown-haired woman stepped in with Michael in her arms. She had been such a comfort in preparing me for Michael's birth. Cathy beamed as she handed him back to me. "Volunteers made these clothes for the babies and I thought you'd want him dressed just like all the other babies."

I was touched when I looked down and saw him cleaned up and dressed. The tiniest white booties I'd ever seen looked like snowshoes on his feet. A small white cap covered his slightly misshapen head. She had even put him in an infant size diaper cut in half and then laid him in a big flannel blanket embroidered with blue feather stitching. I ached to hear him cry, open his eyes, or move, but he limply lay in my arms. He weighed only one pound, two and a half ounces.

"Oh, thank you so much for dressing him. That was so sweet of you. You've been such a help," I weakly added.

Lynne briskly entered, red-eyed and solemn. "Okay, Sue. We'll push your bed down into a vacant room on one of these wings and your relatives can come there and see Michael."

Though she often tried to hide her feelings by joking, there was no laughter in her words today. I hated for her to partake of our sadness, yet I was encouraged that she acknowledged it with tears.

I patted her hand on the edge of the bed as I viewed her stony face. She was restraining her emotions. "It's okay to cry," I reassured her with the same words she had spoken to me a million times during the past few months. She smiled weakly and wiped away a falling tear.

They pushed my bed into a large vacant room filled only with empty beds. Someone had taken Michael from me again. He seemed to age minute by minute. His skin had shaded a darker brown and seemed to stick to the blanket. That view made me feel I was uncomfortably close to holding a dead thing.

Phil's parents, his brother Tim, Holly, David, Mom, Cheryl and Debbie all entered the room with downcast eyes. Lynne stood by to answer any questions while the nurse explained why he should be covered as much as possible. The air was quickly drying out his skin. Reality was hitting everyone. This was a child, a baby, a dying baby. He was part of the family. We must say our hellos and goodbyes in one sentence. I heard David quietly ask why Michael looked so dark and Lynne explained. Holly came to me, now reclining weakly in the bed, and said, "I love you, Mommy." I managed a feeble hug and assured her of my love too.

I wanted to suspend time so I could take a moment to rest, feel better, and then soak in all the macabre happenings when I felt I could handle them. All too soon, the nurse brought Michael to my side for what was to be my last earthly view of him. I wanted to savor the moment. It all seemed like some sick nightmare. My senses were shocked. I hated the finality of it all. My exhaustion now turned to numbness. My head grew dizzy. I gazed at our brown baby without blinking an eye and mechanically said goodbye in my heart.

Everyone left the room as Lynne and another nurse pushed me back into labor and delivery. The harsh realities slapped me in the face, one by one. I was sore and bleeding as from previous deliveries, but this time no living, nursing baby to take my mind off bodily pain and exhaustion. "Sue, do you want to go on the floor with the rest of the new mothers or on the gynecology floor?" a nurse questioned. The thought of listening to crying babies and seeing happy moms comfort them sliced through me like a knife. "Please don't put me with the rest of the mothers. I...I just don't think I could handle it."

Lynne came in and made it official. "Sue, the doctor just checked your baby and he passed away." I looked at the wall clock. Michael Tim had lived exactly two hours and thirty-three minutes. It was 5:12 p.m.

Mom and Phil cautiously surveyed my face as I was wheeled past the floor and nursery full of newborn babies. Soon I was pushed into a room on another floor. A vivacious, bouncing nurse walked in just after Phil fluffed my pillow. She seemed preoccupied, yet friendly.

"Hi! Say, I hope you don't mind. I don't have my charts with me right now. Could you tell me what you're in for?"

"Well, I was pregnant. The baby came early and he died." The jolt of those words pierced me. I never imagined I would ever say, "My baby died." The sentence was like a foreign phrase that needed translation.

The chipper nurse was stunned and speechless. "Oh...uh...oh gee, I'm sorry...uh...I don't know what to say." Mom and Phil awaited my reply along with her.

"It's okay. I know that God has a plan in all of this. It just wasn't His will for Michael to live." I assured her, "You see, I'm hurting right now because I miss him, but I know he's much happier where he is. Sure, I wish he was here, but I know God loves me and He knows what's best." Just verbalizing this seemed to take some of the sting from his death.

A span of silence followed as she cleared her throat and reached out to pat my leg. "Boy, I really needed someone like you today." The tightened lines in her face and brows relaxed. "You wouldn't believe the kind of day I've had, and well, it sure helps to hear someone like you. You know, there's a girl right next door who lost her baby today too, and she's over there crying. I just don't know what to say to her. She's all alone...came down here on vacation to visit her mother, and boom, she goes into labor and loses the baby. She was only about five months along, so her baby didn't have much of a chance either. Would you mind talking to her?"

Though I felt guilty for thinking it, I was comforted to know I wasn't the only one who lost her baby today. "Sure, I'll be glad to go and see her."

Phil and Mom stayed long enough to watch me sparingly eat my meal. A sick feeling was settling in the pit of my stomach. The realities of the day were rushing over me in waves. The grace and strength of a few minutes ago seemed to vanish and a lonely sorrow moved in. The tears began falling again and all of us cried together one more time over the loss of our son and grandchild. We prayed and wearily pulled ourselves together. Without much argument, both Phil and Mom agreed to go home and get some rest. As they walked away, my room seemed the size of a gymnasium. The walls were so cold and inhospitable. I felt more alone than I'd ever known. No human emotion could touch the loneliness that was so dark and solemn. I needed to divert my thoughts, so I forced my legs over the bed and slowly walked to the room of the woman I had promised to encourage.

Still dizzy, I leaned on the doorway and gave a weak knock. There sat a swollen-eyed brown-haired woman, sobbing quietly. I managed a timid word. "May I come in?"

Wiping her tears, she answered, 'Uh, sure."

"I know you don't know me, but my name is Sue. The nurses told me about you and thought maybe you might like someone to talk to. You see, I lost my baby today, too."

I grasped her hand and we shared silent tears. She proceeded to tell me her story and then I told her mine. As we conversed, I realized God's grace was sustaining me and empowering me to do and say things I never thought possible. Slowly, I opened up my grief wound to this stranger. We could both sense the healing going on. We oohed and aahed over Polaroid photos of our lost children. I discovered she was a Christian and encouraged her with thoughts of our babies in heaven.

"Just think. They could be meeting each other right now. Who knows? Maybe they know that we're together too," I added. Though cheered, our fatigue was apparent and I stood up to make my exit.

"I'll stop in and see you later, okay?"

"Please do."

The cool clean hospital sheets were a catharsis for my tired bones. A smile appeared as I thought of God's tender care for me in this situation. "He knew just what I needed," I thought as I drifted into a light catnap.

I was awakened by the light touch of a kind-eyed attractive nurse. "I'm sorry to wake you," she breathed, "but I need to get your temp and blood pressure."

I lay still as she strapped together the velcro strips of the blood pressure cuff and inserted a plastic instrument in my mouth. A coiling cord connected this modern day thermometer to a small box held in her slender hand.

Studying her face, I could sense a tenderness there. I was sure she had read my chart and knew why I was there. "Are you doing all right?" she shyly inquired.

A tear slowly found its way out the corner of my eye making a downy splash on the unblotted sheet. "Yes. I was feeling pretty sad a minute ago. My hand habitually fell on my stomach, and then I realized there was nothing there." More tears. "I'm sure gonna miss my little guy."

I pulled the pictures from the nightstand. "Here's what he looked like. He was so cute."

Carefully, she took the pictures and studied each one. Tears welled up in her pretty brown eyes. "Ah, yes," I thought. "She has a mother's heart." Her show of emotion touched me.

"I'm sorry," she quietly added, as if she were breaking some rule. "I guess I'm not helping you much. It just seems so sad...."

"Hey, don't feel bad for crying. I think I'd feel hurt if you didn't cry. I'm a woman who lost a baby today. I'll never hear his cry or cuddle him in my arms. If you can't grieve with me, that would make it even worse!" I insisted. I shared Michael's story with her and through my tears told her of the peace that God had given me, knowing that He had this all in His plan. He knew what He was doing, He made no mistake. When I finished, more healing had come to my open wound.

"Oh. Thanks for sharing that. I really don't think I could handle it as well as you."

"Well, just remember. God's giving me the grace. I couldn't possibly survive this all on my own." It was my way of using the experience to glorify God. I knew opportunities would come but I was surprised at how quickly. Our conversation ended and she left the room wiping away more tears.

18
Empty Arms

The night was long and strange. The events of the day flashed through my mind in strobe-light fashion. I would awaken in a cold sweat, shaking my head and hoping it was a nightmare. Patting my tummy, I was jolted back to reality. No kicks greeted my searching hand. The soreness of my body reminded me I'd given birth to a child who wasn't there. The unfamiliar surroundings yielded no comfort. As the moon peeked through the crack in the heavy curtain, I realized, "Today is still March ninth, my baby's birthday." The moonlight glistened off the steel bed rails. The sound of amplified voices paging doctors filtered from the hallway into my room. I yearned to see a chubby baby resting in an incubator beside me. My arms craved the heavenly soft touch of newborn skin, yet I hugged only empty air. In the stillness of the moment, loneliness engulfed me.

"Oh Lord," I whispered, "I've never known this kind of awful pain before. Oh, how I wish you could take it away. Why does it have to hurt so? What scares me even more is that I know this is probably only the beginning. I'm frightened, Lord. I feel I'm going to be swallowed up in grief. Please help me. Just help me through this moment. Give me peace so I can sleep." My prayer uttered, release came and I drifted into sleep.

Phil showed up early the next morning. I guessed by his gray- encircled eyes that sleep had escaped him too. Embracing me in a good morning hug, he sighed heavily. His hug was overpowered by heaving sobs. We wept together as we realized we would take no proud bundle home from this hospital visit. Later, Phil confessed he had awakened that morning with the smell of the baby in his nostrils. It was an unexpected emotional symptom of his grief.

I pulled his drawn face into my hands. "I'm so glad you can cry, Honey. I don't know what I'd do if you couldn't show your feelings. Thank you for being such a good husband. I love you so much."

We shared thoughts from the previous day and marveled at God's sustaining power through this difficult time.

Lynne came in. "Are you guys okay?" We assured her we were sad, but "hanging in there." "As you said all along, only God knows. Now, we all know what His answer was, don't we, Lynne?"

Quietly she replied, "Yes, but I wish it could've turned out differently. He was such a little fighter. If he could've just hung on a few more weeks...." We all slipped into private thoughts.

I interrupted the silence, "I went next door and visited another woman who lost her baby yesterday."

"Yeah. Yesterday was a really tough day," Lynne confessed. "We lost three premature babies...yours, the girl's next door, and another woman's in the room to your right. All of the babies were at about the same stage of development."

She completed her exam and told me I could go home. Giving me a final hug, she added, "You be sure and call me if you have any problems or if you just want to talk."

We thanked her for her care and concern and

assured her of our love.

"You know, if it was anyone else except you guys, I'd be more concerned. But I've seen the people from your church. You guys have a super support group there." I knew it would fall on uncomprehending ears to try and explain how the church body functions.

After dressing, I made a quick visit to the couple next door who lost their baby. This was the third couple Lynne had told us about. I knocked at the door's edge and studied two silhouettes etched in the morning light. Explaining our loss of the day before, I asked if there was any way I could help. Both sat slump-shouldered on the edge of the bed and stared coldly at me. They seemed to be in a state of shock. I shifted uneasily on my feet. "Did you get a picture of your baby?"

"No," the husband answered coldly. "We didn't want to see 'it.'" The "it" fell flatly on my ears. Maybe it was easier to deal with death if they depersonalized the baby to an "it." I didn't force the conversation. I wanted to let them work through their grief in their own way. I was already learning a lot about grief and how it affected people.

A nurse was summoned to give me the traditional wheelchair ride out of the hospital. My senses gripped the awesomeness of the moment. I had no baby to hold or take home. There I sat in the wheelchair, holding all the paraphernalia a new mother holds, yet no newly-bundled baby. I felt people's glances. Were the smiling faces searching for the absent baby? Could they read the depth of sorrow on our faces? The ride was soon over and I hurried to crawl into the car.

As we pulled out of the hospital driveway, I started to snap the brown seat belt. The strap rested tightly against a nonpregnant, slightly swollen tummy. My hand absently landed on its familiar resting place. It was different. There was no shelf of baby. The world rushed in—lonely, void of happiness, full of nothing. All I could do was grasp Phil's hand and pour out tears from the depths of my soul.

The trip home was the beginning of many finalities realized. A heavy silence engulfed us as we separately reviewed all our previous trips home. Those voyages were so different; the times when we sang hymns, cried tears of relief. Always, though, we brought our unseen passenger "hope" along with us. This time, our visitor was gone, never to be seated again. Searching Phil's face through the curtain of tears, I saw a broken man. He must be seeing the same flashbacks of previous trips home. This one was so final. We'd be making no more mad dashes. The noise of our wheels seemed to shout, "No baby! No baby!"

We pulled into our familiar parking spot next to the lush green hedge. I steadied myself and started toward the house. I sobbed out to Phil, "All I've got to carry is this crumby box of Kotex!"

As we opened the front door, Mom's tiny arms wrapped around us. We cried together once more. She was there to tend to a wounded, weakened daughter, with no newborn to hold, no baby's smile peeking from behind a blanket in my arms. She felt the emptiness too.

The remainder of the day crept by. Calls came and we numbly answered. It was hard to shake the feeling that this was all just an unreal nightmare.

Some close friends who had also lost their child that year knew our situation. They decisively made all the funeral arrangements for us. They had inquired about what type of arrangements we wanted while I was still in the hospital. We requested others in the church to spread the word. A memorial service would be held on Friday, March 11th. We knew it was soon, but felt we needed to get things over with quickly.

Subconsciously, I deferred additional rest, wanting to forget I had a post-pregnant body. I was determined to buy a nonmaternity dress to wear to the memorial service. Everything in my closet was just too small. Nothing could accommodate my engorged bustline and swollen tummy. Having more determination than strength, I finally convinced a friend to take me to the mall.

With each forced step, my dizziness reminded me I was not physically ready to make this trip. Still, I gritted my teeth. The movements of shoppers seemed frenzied and busy while I felt ragged and sluggish. The world was in fast forward. I was in slow motion. In the midst of the crowds I felt lonely and empty. My eyes riveted to a swollen tummy on a happy pregnant woman. "Don't look, Sue," I told myself. "Don't start thinking about it." Everywhere I turned there seemed to be a pregnant woman or mother with a baby. Tears wet my shoulders as I forged on to the dress shop.

I numbly grabbed several brightly colored dresses and headed for the dressing room. Depression settled in deeper as I pushed my swollen figure into dresses made for normal shapes. My silent friend, Linda, willingly put dresses back and gathered other selections about two sizes bigger. Mechanically, I tried the others on and chose the one that felt most comfortable. I'd given up trying to look nice. As we made the purchase, I studied Linda's face. Her large brown eyes oozed empathy as a slow gentle smile came into view. Without a word, I knew she understood some of my pain. She had lost her mother not long before. "Are you ready to go?" she questioned.

"Yeah," I answered weakly, "let's get back home." The ride home was a silent one. Talking was just too much trouble. There was no way I could possibly

145

explain my emotions anyway. The pain was too deep to be touched by words. Linda helped me to the door and left.

The congregation flew into action and supported us in every way. Meals poured in and our refrigerator bulged. Love was a soothing balm that eased some of our pain. Friends decorated the church for the service and even planned the gathering in our home afterwards. They provided food, flowers and much-needed help. I could only hug people and cry as our wonderful church family ministered to our needs. It was obvious they were hurting right along with us.

Friday my eyes shot open, scanning only darkness. Sunrise was hours away. Pain had summoned an alarm inside me and I realized my milk had come in. Though I had no baby to nurse, my body was going through normal postnatal actions. I stumbled through blackness toward the silver moonlight trickling through the living room window. Slumping in a heap beside the window sill, I cried mournfully.

"Oh Lord, this pain is so hard. Did You have to remind me again that I have no baby? Why did You let my milk come in today of all days? This awful day when I have to bury my dear little one. Oh Lord, how I long to hold him and nurse him. Oh God, my arms are so empty!"

I scanned the black sky with the stars shimmering like white Christmas lights. I imagined the Lord looking down and seeing this tiny speck of humanity He created. He could see my heart breaking. He could feel my loss and pain. I could sense His comfort, His arms enveloping me in love. He seemed to say, "Yes, my daughter. I truly know your emptiness and pain. Remember, I gave up my Son, Jesus, to die on the cross. I saw Him suffer a horrible, painful death. But what came after, child? He didn't stay in the ground. He rose up from the dead and because of that, even your little one has eternal life." I imagined Him opening His strong arms, revealing my smiling child, Michael.

Slowly I rose from my knees and quietly crept back to bed. Snuggling next to Phil's sleeping form, I longed for his words of reassurance. I pushed back the temptation to awaken him. "No," I reasoned, "it would be selfish. He needs all the rest he can get. Today will be tough enough. I'll need his strength later more than now."

I felt as though I were lying on hard rocks. The baby's milk in my body demanded to be released. "Maybe if I turn on my back...oh, no. The heaviness is worse. I think it's time for a warm shower." I slipped from the bed and tiptoed to the beige formica shower, The soothing heat of the warm water triggered the let-down reflex. Precious milk streamed out. Grief's vice-like grip seized me. "Soon all reminders of you will be gone, Michael. You can never drink of this life-giving milk. You are dead. You aren't here with me. I'll never have the joy of seeing your little eyes peep out from my breast. The smile of satisfaction from a full tummy will never be yours. I wonder what you're doing now. Do you eat in heaven? Are you a baby or a full-grown man? Do you know how much I miss you? How much I wish I could've known you?"

My tears mingled with the shower water. I stared at the diamond pattern in the beige floor as water pulsed down my back. Invisible tears and water swept down the drain. That river was joined by a thin white stream of milk. Sidy by side, the differing fluids trickled around the diamond pattern, then into the silver drain. "What a waste," I mumbled. The futility of the situation engulfed me. My mother's heart screamed. "Oh Lord! Couldn't You have let me hold him a little while longer? Couldn't I have nursed him just once?" I thrust my face heavenward. Water assaulted my eyes as I fought to stare a hole in the formica ceiling. My view was blurred and things started spinning. Clinging to the slippery wall, I eased myself against it for support and pushed in the silver knob to shut off the water. Weakness and fatigue rudely fought for attention. Postpartum recovery and grief didn't mix. Grabbing a towel off the rack, I thought, "I gotta try and rest."

19
The Graveside

With only a few hours of sleep, I wearily made my way to the kitchen. Mom heard the dishes rattling and arose in a sleepy haze to make breakfast. It was March 11th.

"Good morning, Hon." Her tiny arms engulfed me in a hug. Releasing her hold, she stroked my tousled hair. Food really held no appeal, but I dutifully gulped down breakfast.

"Well, today's the big event," I thought. "Life will soon get back to normal after this service. The 'hold button' will be released. I sure hope I'm ready for all of this." My thoughts drifted. "I wonder what it will be like today. How am I going to feel? Will I be able to talk to people? Will I cry? This is so weird. I'm used to going to funerals and giving people pats on their backs and comforting words." I sighed.

I often wondered how people felt on the day of their loved one's funeral. "Hey, I've got an idea! Why don't I write a letter and give it out at the service. That way everyone will know what's in my heart. It might spare me some tough moments too."

Mom continued to be the short order cook for the rest of the awakening family. I got up and rifled through the desk drawer for a scrap of paper. Leafing through my Bible, I found the perfect verse for the beginning of the letter. "Before I was born, the Lord called me, from my birth He has made mention of my name...yet what is due me is in the Lord's hand, and my reward is with my God" Isaiah 49:1b, 4b.

Dear friends and loved ones:

Thank you for coming to share with us during this time of our grief and our joy. Today, March 11, 1983, we are remembering the birth of Michael Tim Engelman on March 9th. His life was a brief few hours, and yet, in that short time he managed to give us great pleasure by his presence and we truly thank our Father for that. Even though we will miss him greatly, we are so happy that he is now in heaven with his Creator Father and his two brothers or sisters that went before him.

As his mother, there are many precious thoughts stirring within me and I'd like to share a few with you.

From the moment of conception, Phil and I gave him to the Lord, so we have never ever felt the right to selfishly claim him as ours. We went through many difficult times, both physically and emotionally, as we were reminded of this during my pregnancy.

Some may think that my five and half months of suffering was a waste. Others would like to forget that he and his two brothers or sisters were people with living souls. But none of these things are true. God, in His Word, said, "The Lord will fulfill His purpose for me" Psalm 138:8a. Michael and our other two children definitely enriched our lives and the lives of others. Yes, they brought to us much joy and served their purpose. Again and again I draw comfort from Psalm 139 and know "Your eyes saw my unformed body; all the days for me were written in Your book before one of them came to be" Psalm 139:16. They all were human beings with living souls.

I know in time God will heal these wounds of grief

and pain, but I'm assured that I will never ever forget Michael and his two brothers or sisters, just as I cannot presently forget my other three gifts from God—Holly, David and Jonathan.

The greatest truth of all is that God has not forgotten us. He knows our pain, for He gave up His only Son in a far different manner than I gave my children. Michael and the others died peacefully and with those who loved them. Jesus suffered a cruel death at the hands of His very creation who refused to admit He was their God. They hated Him and rejected Him, yet He looked in love and died for us, even while we were yet sinners.

"Can a mother forget the baby at her breast and have no compassion on the child she has borne? Though she may forget, I will not forget you! See, I have engraved you on the palms of my hands" Isaiah 49:15-16a.

Just as I will never forget this day, or you, I pray you will never forget God who eternally remembers us all and gave His Son, Jesus Christ, to display His love. He gave us all this special day to share. Thank you for being here.

> In His Joy and Peace,
> Sue

With my signature written, release poured forth and more healing soothed my wound. I called Phil into the bedroom. Thrusting the paper into his hand, I asked, "Here, would you read this?"

"Sure," he answered hastily and began reading. His eyes filled with misty tears as he looked up. My fingers touched his eyes and wiped the tears away. "That's...good," he stammered, "it's really good." Emotion caught us once again. We choked back the flow. "We can't do this now," Phil interjected. "It'll be a long day."

A knock at the living room door summoned us and my dad walked in along with my younger brother, John, and his wife, Kathy.

"Hi, you guys," I forced cheerfully. "Come on in."

My ever-quiet brother, John, hugged me. "Hi." Kathy gave a shy downward glance and joined in the hug.

Dad's gnarled carpenter hand pressed my shoulder. Silent words too precious to utter were exchanged. I slipped from John and Kathy's hug and engulfed myself in Dad's arms. I pressed my face into his shoulders as I sought comfort like a little girl. Years were removed as I looked up from Dad's strong shoulders into his soft blue eyes. "Thanks for coming, Dad."

I studied his time-worn face. His cleft chin jutted out handsomely complimenting his deep dimples. A slow smile came. "I know, Sis." He released me after an emphatic hug.

Phil struggled to get the kids all dressed while Mom hustled in the kitchen making coffee. "Who's going to be here at the house while we're at the graveside?"

"Lots of the women in the church are coming over to set up coffee, drinks and food. I really don't know much about it. Marilyn's been super. She and Cheryl got everything organized. You wouldn't believe how beautifully they decorated the church. I slipped over there yesterday and I was really touched by all the special care they took."

Unsure of our feelings on this day, Phil and I previously arranged that only family and a small group of friends be present at the graveside. We wanted a private time to be with loved ones.

The hour was approaching, so I needed to get ready. "I wonder if I'll cry all this make-up off," I thought. "You better use tons of concealer toay, Sue.

Boy, have you got circles under those eyes." Maybe to some it seemed silly to try to look my best. Habits die hard and a pastor's wife learns to get through some of the toughest moments that life hands out. This was no different.

Slipping the electric-purple dress over my head, I winced at my reflection in the mirror. "Boy, this purple is really bright. I wonder if people will think this is a little out of place." My internalization stopped. "Well, I guess I just don't care. I don't want to look all sad and morose today. The situation's bad enough as it is. Besides," I laughed, "it has black trim at the arms and waist." Placing a purple flower in my curls, I stood back and took a critical look. "One thing about this dress—it sure camouflages my swollen body. It's nice not to look pregnant."

Searching for cologne in our closet, I heard the familiar thud of a car door closing outside. Our bathroom window overlooked the church parking lot. I stood on the toilet seat and peeped out the high window struggling to see who had arrived. The slightly balding head of my oldest brother, Mike, breezed past. "What? That couldn't be Mike! He lives six hours away!"

"Mom!" I called as I burst from our bedroom door. "You won't believe it! Mike's here!"

Dad's ever-calm expression changed to mild surprise. Before Mike could knock twice, I flung open the door.

"You nut! What are you doing here? You didn't have to come!"

"Well, I wanted to be here, Sis. It's the least I could do."

I grabbed him in a spontaneous hug. "But's it's such a long trip, Mike. When did you leave?"

"I drove all night. Left about midnight." A mischievous smile broke the solemnity. "Took a bunch of coffee and lots of tapes. Listened to some great sermons. Kind feel like I had my own little revival. Before I knew it, I was here!"

Nervous giggles filled the air. It felt good to smile and laugh. My thoughts drifted back through the years. Mike, big brother Mike. He always had played the part well. I was the admiring little sister. My girlfriends were always impressed with his good looks, chestnut hair, rugged manly features. His baby blue eyes, dimpled smile and cleft chin added to his attractiveness. Dry wit was his forte. Even now, he used it to lighten us up and add joy.

A wave of family love swept over me. My eyes riveted to his. "Mike," I spoke tenderly, "you'll never know how much this means to me." We all sat there, speaking a wordless language. Grief enveloped us in a bittersweet wave. We didn't resist. No tears came for even they were held back. I seized the love I felt in this moment and sealed it in an invisible bottle. I reasoned, "I'll need to pull this out and drink of it often during these next few weeks." A knock again broke the silence. Women from the church entered in hushed tones and began preparing the tables.

"Mommy. Isn't it about time to go?" Holly questioned, breaking the silence.

"Yeah. I guess so. You go get David. Jonathan will stay here with the ladies."

The crackle of wood burning in the franklin stove reminded me of the cool weather. A cold snap left us with unseasonably brisk air for March. Goosebumps signaled a need for more clothing. I rushed to my closet and pulled out a black velvet blazer.

"Oh, Sue," Mom fussed. "I feel so embarrassed. I have such a crazy outfit on. I wasn't really prepared for all this. I hope I won't embarrass you."

"Oh, don't be silly, Mom. People won't care," I

reassured. "You know it's really cold outside. You better wear something warmer."

"This is all I had in my suitcase."

"Here," I offered, "wear my cape. I won't need it." Mom gladly accepted and we left. David, Holly, Phil and I rode in one car. The others rode separately.

The graveside was only two minutes away from the house. Seated in the front, I stared out the car window. It was overcast and drizzling.

Breathing deeply, a slow heavy sigh seaped from my lips. "Wouldn't you know it would rain. Perfect funeral weather."

"Yeah," Phil agreed.

Pulling around the bend, I could see a group of tall pine trees ahead with green canvas-backed chairs in their midst. Like a magnet my eyes riveted to the tiny white satin covered casket. A large spray of white daisies and babies breath covered the lid. The car stopped. I took another deep breath and forced my legs outside the car.

The casket, though only about two feet long, was all I could see. Indescribable pain lashed my soul like a whip. My cruel torturer, grief, laid his hardest blows. "This is only the beginning," he hissed.

Phil tenderly helped me into the green seat, settling the children next to me. I was oblivious to those behind me. All I could see was the casket.

In hushed tones, the funeral director spoke with Phil. Soon he stepped aside and Phil began. Skillfully, Phil presented the promises in God's Word. He emphasized Michael's aliveness in heaven with the Lord. I studied the face of this gentle, wise man God had blessed me with. No touch of despair etched lines in his forehead. Godly contentment and peace filled his visage. I drew from that source of strength and pain subsided.

155

Winds continued to bite our warmth. The kids snuggled closer searching for shelter from the cold. They looked like little waifs. Their eyes were so wide and filled with confusion. It was hard for them to comprehend my sadness over a brother they'd never known.

The service ended and I tapped my fingernails on the black camera I held in my hands. Pointing at it I mouthed, "Phil, don't forget the pictures."

"I know this seems unusual," Phil explained to the small group of fourteen, "but Sue and I wanted to get a picture of you."

I squeezed my fingers tighter around my coat. Click, click. I managed a hypocritical smile. Click. More views of the casket. "Thanks, everyone. We'll meet you back at the house."

One car door after another thudded till silence came again. Phil, the funeral director and the kids looked on while I stood next to the casket. "Stay right there, Hon, and maybe we can get another picture. The man in the dark black suit clicked the button. "Thanks," Phil added.

I longed to see Michael just once more. A new thought hit me. "I never kissed him. I wonder...would it be sick of me to kiss him?" I envisioned myself prying off the lid and sweeping up my sweet baby in my arms and kissing him.

"Is there any way I could see him?" I asked the funeral director.

"I'm sorry. He...he just was in such bad shape," he stammered.

"You mean he's already started to decompose?" I boldly questioned.

Slowly he confirmed, "Yes, I'm sorry."

"That's okay," I answered. I stretched out my fingers and caressed the daisies on the casket. Each finger searched for a baby's warm chubby skin but found only daisies. Agony crept from fingers to heart, finding a vulnerable target. I gasped for air. Hot tears blurred my view.

"Oh, if only...if only I could just kiss him, just hold him one more time," I whispered in a small voice.

"What?" Phil questioned. He slipped his arm around my waist, then grabbed my hand.

Leaning my dizzy head on his shoulder I confessed. "I long to hold him so much, Honey. I never thought I'd live long enough to see a piece of my flesh shoved into the ground."

"I know," he consoled as he stroked my hair. "Come on. We better go now." The kids stared at me, eyes wide.

I hated to leave. That meant one more finality. More and more of Michael gone. Compelling my feet to obey, I took one last look through the rain-drizzled windshield. His tiny casket seemed so minute next to the tall pines. "Goodby, Michael," I whispered as we pulled away.

20
A Long Day

We came home to a sweltering house. The good old wood stove had taken the house from cozy to unbearable. Sweat dripped from the ladies' brows who had been patiently waiting for us to arrive from the graveside. They were all too polite to say anything. Eveyone surveyed our faces and glanced down. Pain was easy to see.

Phil lightened the awkward moment. "Hey! Aren't you guys roasting? Goodness, it must be a hundred ten in here! Let's open the doors and windows!" Crisp air swooshed in and made things bearable.

Food overflowed the counters and tables. Everywhere I looked there were desserts, cakes, sandwiches and vegetables. The kids delightedly gulped food and enjoyed the extra company. We purposely set aside two hours before the service for people to come by and express their sympathy. I wanted to see everyone before the service so I could be alone afterwards.

One by one, friends started arriving. Mom cradled my arm and pulled me over. "I'm afraid Dad wants to leave now, Honey," Mom whispered.

"You're kidding!" I gasped. "You mean he won't stay for the service?"

"I'm sorry, Honey. You don't know how much I want

158

to stay.... I just don't think he can handle it. You know your father."

"That's okay, Mom. Yeah. I think I understand. I don't really agree, but I understand. I sure wish we could talk about it. I really need him today, but, well, I love him anyway. Maybe some day we'll be able to talk about it. For now, I'll let him handle it in his own way. I love you, Mom." I squeezed her tightly. "I know this is hard on you. Try and get some rest."

Dad sheepishly came alongside us. His hand squeezed my shoulder. "Well, Sis, we're gonna have to go now. I've got several things I've gotta do when I get home. So we better be gettin' home before the heavier traffic."

"Thanks again for coming, Dad. It meant a lot."

As they exited, Mom glanced back giving a pained "I wish I could stay, but my place is with him" look. I nodded in acknowledgment and blew her a goodbye kiss.

A sea of faces came and packed into our hot living room. One after another expressed their sympathy. I looked up from a friend's embrace and saw Lynne's familiar blonde curls. Her wide blue eyes were rimmed with red. I sensed she was holding back tears.

Giving me a hug she whispered, "How're ya doin'?"

I gave her hands a reassuring squeeze. "Hey, what can I say? I'm hangin' in there. Thanks so much for coming. I know how busy you are...." I glanced at my watch. "Well, I guess we better be getting over to the church. It's time. Holly, why don't you walk Miss Lynne over and show her where to go?"

Holly grinned shyly and grabbed Lynne's hand. "Sure, Mom, I'll show her." Soon they were heading out the door with everyone else.

My heart throbbed. I was glad for the moment of silence after everyone left.

Gathering deep breaths of air, I asked God for strength. "Well, Lord, this is it. Only you can get me through this."

Phil's familiar arm held my shoulders again. We walked wordlessly to the church. I purposely waited until the last few moments so I wouldn't have a long wait before the service began. Phil went around the back entrance while I slipped in the side door. Quietly, I found my lone spot on the front pew and the service began. My eyes fell on the carefully placed picture of Michael Tim in a gold frame. It was sitting on a table surrounded by flowers and lighted candles. Jo, the church pianist, was playing a beautiful prelude. Sweet notes of "Jesus Loves Me, This I Know" brought tugs on my heart. "Oh, if only Jesus hadn't loved him quite so much," I reasoned, "then Michael would be here now."

The rest of the service was a bittersweet blur. Phil's sermon brought comfort, yet part of me cried. Surprisingly, tears never flowed. I felt numb, emotionless. Phil and I walked to the back of the church to say goodbye to people. Many slipped away without facing us. I knew it was too hard for them. Others provided sweet comfort with just tears and "I'm so sorry, you guys. I don't really know what to say. I'm praying for you."

Over and over we heard, "You guys are doing so well. You're so strong." I grew more confused. I knew I wasn't strong. I could still hardly believe this was happening to us.

Making our way home, we were greeted with a rich roast beef aroma as we entered the door. "Mm-m," I licked, "that meat smells great. Alva must've left her food, Honey." Hunger jumped from nowhere. All I wanted to do now was eat. Hurriedly I set the food on the table. Our family sat there together enjoying the home-cooked meal in silence.

We pushed from the table stuffed, yet feeling so empty. "I can't fill this emptiness with food. I wonder if this awful, painful hurt will ever heal."

We tucked each child in bed. Grudgingly, I admitted exhaustion. "C'mon, Honey. Let's see if we can get some sleep. It's been a long day."

21
A Pain Called Grief

Days ticked by, second by second. The gnawing, knife-like pain refused to leave. Grief was lacing its fingers around my throat and choking me into reality. The finalities of death gripped me more and more. I'd go to the grocery store and come home sobbing because I saw a woman in the line buying diapers. News of a heart recipient dying brought inappropriate resentment. "The whole world knows he's dead and yet not many know Michael died."

The Sunday following the memorial service, I faithfully parked myself in the front pew at church. To avoid conversation with anyone I made another late entrance. Though I participated in the hymn singing, I was merely a body filling a pew. A genuine smile was an impossibility. The emptiness and loneliness yanked any comfort from me. I was merely a "Sunday robot" going through the motions. My heart was gone. I felt eyes staring. I wished I'd never come.

Phil came to the platform, "I want to thank you all for your tremendous support of Sue and me these last few months. As you may have heard, our son, Michael Tim Engelman, was born March 9th and died two hours later. It's hard to believe he was twenty-three weeks along in development. It shocked us that he was only one week away from the time most clinics shy away from doing abortions. He was so tiny and perfect...."

His voice was interrupted by my anger. "How dare he use Michael as a topic for a sermon point? How come he just stood up there and talked with no tears?" My illogical anger surprised me. Pushing the unwanted emotion away, I forced my attention to Phil's sermon. Five minutes from quitting time, I slipped out during prayer and walked home.

I felt so vulnerable and broken. Tissue paper had more strength. I was ripped in all directions. "What in the world is wrong with me? Am I going crazy?" I opened my Bible. The pages merely held words with no meaning. I couldn't even pray.

Mom came back from Lake Wales that afternoon to be with me a couple more days. Wisely she suggested I stay home from the evening service. Phil agreed. Everyone left for church. We had the evening alone.

"Oh, Mom. I've got the tape of the memorial service. Would you like to hear it?"

"I'd love to. But are you sure it wouldn't bother you too much?"

"No, I'd like to hear it again," I assured, switching on the tape player.

For the next half hour we shared the service. With the click of the tape we ended our silence and joined tears. I stroked her hand. "It's all right, Mom. Go ahead. Let it out." The "go" button pushed, a torrent of deep soul tears fell. "I'm s-s-sorry, Honey. I g-g-guess I was holding it all in. Y-you know, trying to be strong for you. But I guess I just realized that I've lost a little grandson."

Her grief comforted me. I needed to know someone else was sad he was gone. "Oh Mom, I miss him so much. It's hard to describe how empty I feel right now. My arms long to cradle a baby. Oh Mom, the pain's so deep. I never knew it would be this bad!"

She threw her arms around me. We hugged until

we had no more strength. Feeling cleansed, we gained composure and spoke tenderly of our missing baby. Weariness crept in.

"I think we need some rest," Mom added. "Do you need anything before we go to bed?"

"No, I'll be all right. Thanks for coming, Mom. I love you so much!" We ended our time with another bear hug and went to our separate rooms.

Climbing into bed, I was struck by the dreaded thought, "Sue, this is only the beginning. Grief isn't a pretty thing. It's like an open gash. It'll take time. The cut has just been made."

The next few days proved this true. Instead of getting better, I felt worse. It was a good thing Mom was there that first week. Decisions were almost impossible for me to make. No two thoughts seemed to connect. I felt loose-ended. Uncharacteristically, I craved sweets. Usually, I stayed away from desserts and junk food, but now I longed for them.

I knew it was time for Mom to leave. The reattached apron strings had to be cut. She'd been such a comfort with her soft-spoken ways. For one week we forgot time and became mother and daughter of years past. It was time to come back to face realities.

"It's gonna be hard not to think of that room as 'Nanny Gardner's room.' We sure will miss you, but I know it's time for you to leave. Tell Dad I said, 'hi.'" I sensed my control slipping. "I don't think I'll walk you to the car, Mom. I love you. Have a safe trip home."

I shut the door, closing the four-foot-eleven-inch form from my sight. Tears streamed from my eyes. I hated these goodbyes. "Oh Lord, sometimes this life is so hard. I'm so sick of goodbyes. First Michael, now Mom. I hate the pain love brings. Help me get through this day."

Two weeks went by. I was such a good actress at

church. Everyone continued to admire my strength. "Didn't they recognize the glazed look of shock?" I analyzed my feelings and became my own judge and jury. "You're definitely ungodly and unspiritual for all these feelings, Sue. Don't you dare tell Phil or anyone else. Don't let them know how awful you feel. It'll only depress them. If you even hinted you thought of suicide they'd be upset." Grief was like a cavity, eating away my "enamel." I pretended its presence wasn't there but the cavity only grew.

I talked less. Laughter was gone. Nothing brought joy. Life seemed so pointless. I buried my head in my pillow. "Oh, God! Please take this awful pain away. Let me get on with life! Can't you remove this nightmarish agony? Oh please, please help!" My muffled sobs were still loud enough for Phil to hear from the other room.

He entered, sat next to the bed, reached for my arm, and turned me over. My reddened, puffy eyes stared angrily at him. "What? What do you want?" I snapped like a cornered and wounded animal.

He pulled away. His previous gentleness turned into impatience. "What's wrong with you? How long is this gonna go on?"

"What do you mean?" I flashed.

"I mean, good grief! It's been two weeks! You should be over this by now!"

"Oh Honey, I'm so scared! I don't know what's wrong. I hurt so bad. I want this whole grief thing to go away and be over with, but it won't! I've even thought of killing myself! I mean, the pain just hurts so. I just want to escape it."

Shock flashed across his face. "Hon, I think we need to get away. I'll arrange everything. Let's just go somewhere where we can talk. I'm sorry I didn't do it before now. I guess I just didn't realize how bad you were. I'm sorry." He buried his head in my shoulder and cried.

"It still hurts too much to feel," I reasoned, "so I'm just gonna shut all my emotions off." My blank stare continued while Phil waited for a return hug. I couldn't give it.

"That's okay, Hon. You're gonna be all right. I'm going to make arrangements now." He left the room while I laid there like a stone mummy.

The following morning after the kids went to school Phil announced his plans. "It's all taken care of. We're going on a little trip, today."

"What? Where are we going? Oh, I don't want to go anywhere. I don't want to pack. Why'd you do this?"

"Aw, c'mon," Phil soothed, "you'll enjoy yourself. I've arranged for people to watch the kids. I want you to just throw a few things together. Let's go!"

Not giving much thought to what I grabbed, I quickly packed. Soon we were speeding toward the interstate in silence. Anger in me grew. Stubbornness sealed my lips. "Okay," I thought, "he may get me away, but I'm not gonna talk." Phil just ignored the nonverbal signals my tightly folded arms and gritted teeth were sending.

Reaching over to my leg, he affectionately patted my knee. "So, Honey, how are you doing today?"

I gave him an icy stare. Silence. Undaunted, he ventured, "Don't you wonder where we're going?"

More silence.

"C'mon, Honey. It's not gonna do you any good to clam up. C'mon. I want to help you. I love you. Please talk."

"So just what do you expect of me this weekend?" I angrily shot back. He knew my underlying thought. We had been sleeping in the same bed, but we were like roommates instead of lovers. We had not come together since before Michael was born. The doctors had warned that the risk of infection was too high.

Phil patiently replied, "I expect absolutely nothing. Honey, if all we do is talk, it's fine with me. I'm putting no pressure on you for anything. I just want you to know you're loved."

His answer brought relief and disarmed me. "How could any woman have a husband this patient?" I thought. "Well, uh, where are we going?" I sheepishly questioned.

"I don't really know!" he cheerfully quipped. "I thought we'd just drive till we got tired of talking and then find a nice motel and spend the night. We'll eat out, watch TV in the room and sleep in late. We'll head back tomorrow."

City streets and cement buildings passed. Soon we viewed green orange groves and lush meadows. Phil, with a sensitivity to the Holy Spirit, asked one question after another. "What surprised you the most about grief?" "What did you think of the hospital care?" "Who do you want to thank the most?" "What comments hurt?" "What helped?" As he asked, my wound of grief was lanced. The pus oozed out. I shared my deepest thoughts. The more I talked, the better I felt. Healing crept in. A new awareness of Phil's presence excited me. My fingers searched for his hand and squeezed.

"I love you, Hon," I cooed. "How did God ever bless me with a man like you?"

The rest of the day gently passed. We stopped at Weeki-Wachi Springs and giggled at the mermaids. Luscious gardens bedecked with bright flowers reflected the wonders of God's beauty in creation. We found a nice motel nearby and relaxed a while. As usual, TV didn't have much to offer. As we prepared for bed, I felt tranquilized by the days events. A tinge of longing for Phil returned for the first time in months. With the lights off, we gently became one again. I wasn't prepared for the rush of emotions. The very act that brought such joy, now brought emotional pain. Michael's conception had been so happy.

Now again, the finalities hit me. Michael was gone. Phil patiently cradled me in his arms. "It's okay, Honey. I know how you feel...."

"Hon, I'm so scared. Do you think these thoughts will come to me every time we're together now? Will Michael forever ruin our love life?" I asked.

"No, Sue. Don't worry. I've read that this is normal after an infant death. Be patient. Time will heal this wound."

His incredible understanding amazed me. What a love gift this man was! Truly this trial in our lives had brought us much closer together.

"I love you, Phil." I fell asleep in his arms and had one of the most restful times in weeks.

Early morning came and we hungrily ate a large breakfast. The rolling hills and green groves startled me with their beauty. Colors were more vibrant. An invisible fog had lifted. Hopelessness was replaced with hope. The first scar tissue was forming on my wound. Life wasn't as pointless. Placing my head on Phil's shoulder, I sighed happily. "Oh, Honey, thank you so much for this trip. I think I'm finally ready to face life without Michael."

With a twinkle in his eye, Phil beamed devilishly. "Mm-m, ready for another baby yet?"

I slapped him on the back. "You nut!" And our laughter filled the car and the world around us. God was filling my empty arms with my husband, children and Himself. Maybe, in the future, He'd fill them with a baby.

Epilogue

Yes, God had His plans for Sue and Phil. Three months later, Sue became pregnant again. They were still trying for that fourth and final child. She started bleeding in the third month. Sue and Phil both wondered if they could possibly be reliving the former nightmare. But a few weeks later, the bleeding stopped for good.

In her fifth month, Sue developed mysterious hives. They appeared during her twenty-third week, the same point at which Michael had died in the previous pregnancy. The hives were persistent, huge, and carried a maddening twenty-four-hour-a-day itch. Though she consulted allergists and other doctors, the only way she could obtain a measure of relief was to stay on constant medication throughout the remainder of the pregnancy. In spite of great concern on the part of the doctors over any effect the medication might have on the baby, Sue gave joyful birth amidst hives to a perfectly healthy girl—Abigail Lynne Engelman, a child who would've never been born had it not been for the passing of Michael Tim.

After Abby's birth, the hives faded and the Engelmans now have four beautiful children, two boys and two girls.

Appendix A
Practical Pointers

Having experienced the trauma of miscarriage and stillbirth and having counselled others, I have learned some practical lessons. May I offer the following suggestions to those who might be in a position to counsel or offer support to those who may have had similar experiences:

1. Never expect two people to react in exactly the same way.

I have observed a remarkable variety of responses in women who have experienced miscarriage:

a. some experience irrational guilt. Questions about the possibility that greater care taken during the pregnancy may have saved the baby are a common experience for many women. For example, there are some who become convinced due to the timing of the loss that sexual intercourse brought on the miscarriage.

b. some women experience very little grief or emotional trauma. This reaction is most common in first time and early miscarriage experiences. Women who genuinely do not grieve or grieve very little should not be made to feel guilty for responding in this way. Of course, this reaction is not to be confused with the problem of concealing a deep hurt under a cheerful facade.

c. some become bitter and depersonalize the baby. This is a defense mechanism that may be erected in order to deal with the emotional hurt. Some couples refuse to name the baby or refer to the child as "it."

2. Never set a time limit on grief.

Everyone seems to have his or her own preconceived deadlines on how long a person should grieve after a loss. In some cases, people do wallow in self-pity, but the solution is not to demand they "snap out of it." Like an emotional sickness, grief has to run its course and there is a great variety of patterns among individuals. Some who genuinely want to recover from their depression continue in it for a prolonged period. They often feel guilt for not "getting over it" which only compounds the depression. A counsellor who can draw out the person to express their honest feelings can do much toward healing the emotional wounds.

3. Never feel obligated to provide answers.

Quite often, the person in grief is not looking for theological answers. Her greatest immediate needs may simply be a listening ear and an understanding heart. Many times a wordless hug or tear shed in response is sufficient to provide comfort. Biblical truths are precious and need to be applied at the right times and in the right way, but one should not always feel compelled to have something to say. Sometimes people are guilty of presuming on God by the answers given about the whys, wherefores and outcomes of life's difficulties. Patience and silence may be the best policy.

4. Never minimize the loss as a means of comfort.

Comments like, "Oh, you'll have another. You're still young. Just think of how much fun you'll have trying for another one," or "At least you weren't further along in your pregnancy," don't provide any real comfort. Usually the woman in grief has already looked for the bright side. Statements like these only communicate that her emotional pain is not understood.

5. Never avoid or change the subject.

When a person grieves, it is natural for them to want to speak of the loss. Too often friends are under the mistaken impression that to bring up the subject will open old wounds. The fact is, talking about the loss is a means toward healing the grief. Often the discomfort as a friend comes from the fear that in bringing up the subject the wrong things might be said. But if an atmosphere of acceptance can be established where the woman in grief feels free to talk a great service will have been rendered. It is not necessary to provide verbal comfort. A person's very presence is often sufficient encouragement.

6. Never remain invisible.

Don't assume the grieving person wants to be left alone. Often a person in grief has a need for companionship that goes much deeper than during other times in her life. The individual may not request company, but company can often provide the kind of comfort the woman in grief needs. Remember, a listening ear goes a long way to heal a broken heart.

7. Never deny tears.

There is a tendency in all of us to avoid tears, first in ourselves and then in others. People try to hold back tears for fear of stirring up the emotions of the one who is already grieving. In reality, when the grieving person sees tears in the eyes of a friend, she knows she is loved. She knows her friend feels some of the hurt, and that is comforting. Romans 12:15 says, "...weep with those who weep." The discomfort one feels when the grieving person starts crying is the result of a mistaken conclusion. It is assumed that tears show failure as a comforter only making matters worse. Nothing could be further from the truth. Tears are God's mechanism toward emotional healing. Tears may be serving as the catalyst to help the griever deal with the loss.

8. Never assume only the woman grieves.

The tendency to forget the husband's grief is a common one. Though men frequently show less emotion outwardly, my experience indicates they often hurt equally as deeply or nearly as deeply as the woman. Granted, he has not experienced the physical trauma, but most husbands enter into their wives physical trauma vicariously. He has lost the baby in every way his wife has except physically. Bearing this fact in mind will be a valuable tool in counselling.

9. Never offer spiritual counsel before communicating love.

Nothing sounds more hollow than spiritual platitudes offered by a passive observer. To be sure, a woman in grief needs to hear the truth of God that comes to bear on her present situation, but one needs to earn the right to be heard. Until the mourner is given time to talk and express her grief in a nonjudgmental atmosphere, she won't be ready to listen to counsel. Until one has done all possible to express unconditional love, corrective counsel should be avoided.

SOME POSITIVE ADVICE

10. Take initiative in helping make decisions when

circumstances warrant.

In the case of stillbirth, the couple might need help in making funeral arrangements. Decisions are often hard to make when a person is in a state of grief or emotional shock. Any help you can initiate to provide meals, care for the family, or meet any other need will be a great encouragement. One word of caution: be certain to obtain the couple's permission before taking any action.

11. Be sensitive to the physical changes the woman's body is undergoing.

A woman who miscarries or gives birth to a lifeless child experiences far more than the emotional trauma. Because her body has prepared itself for giving birth, there are hormonal adjustments that must take place before returning to normal. In a routine pregnancy, mother has the baby to distract her from the physical discomforts that accompany the postpartum condition. In the case of stillbirth, she has to experience the withdrawal of a body prepared to nurse a child. The accompanying pain makes the reality of her empty arms that much more vivid.

12. Encourage the couple to name the child.

Anything a friend or counsellor can do to encourage a couple to realize it was a real human being they lost will be helpful. Later on in life, they will be glad they gave their child the maximum amount of respect at the time of his death. Often the decision to withhold a name is part of a denial for the sake of dealing with the emotional pain of the loss. If the parents don't know the child's sex at time of death, they could use a "sexless" name like Erin, etc.

13. Be prepared to deal with confusing emotions.

As in all forms of grief, miscarriage and stillbirth bring a torrent of mixed and conflicting emotions to women. Often irrational resentment will surface during the period of readjustment immediately following the shock of the loss. For instance, she may resent women with healthy babies. She may experience the desire to have company while at the same time wanting to be left alone. She may want to be intimate with her husband, but then experience strange emotions upon resuming sexual relations. Her appetite may be altered so she craves food she normally doesn't eat. These are just a few of the confusing emotions the grieving person may experience.

14. Encourage the one in grief to talk.

Even though this subject has been dealt with in points two, five and nine, it certainly deserves its own special comment. From my experience and from counselling others, I have learned that the verbal expressions of what one is truly feeling is the single most important ingredient in the healing of grief. If much time passes without improvement in the one who has suffered the loss, one should do everything possible to help her express whatever emotions she is feeling. If a family member or friend cannot successfully draw her out, then the help of a pastor or professional counsellor may be in order.

Appendix B
Scriptural Truths That Heal

1. Children who die are with the Lord.
   II Samuel 12:23

2. Children's days are predetermined by the Lord.
   Psalm 139:16

3. Children are people even before they are born.
   Psalm 139:13–15

4. We have no right to quarrel with our Maker.
   Isaiah 45:9–12

5. God desires good for us.
   Jeremiah 29:11, Romans 8:28

6. God takes note of our grief.
   Psalm 56:8 cf Malachi 3:16, Isaiah 49:15

7. God understands our grief.
   Hebrews 4:15,16, John 11:33–36

8. God promises to bring us through.
   Lamentations 3:31–33, II Corinthians 4:17

9. God will give us a future glory and reward that
   surpasses our present suffering.
   Romans 8:18, James 1:12, II Corinthians 4:17

10. God promises to one day remove all our sorrow.
    Revelation 21:4, Isaiah 35:10

11. Our suffering is not unique.
    I Corinthians 10:13

12. Our suffering can be used to comfort others.
    II Corinthians 1:3-5

13. Our suffering can offer us an opportunity to learn
    dependence on the Lord.
    II Corinthians 12:9, Isaiah 40:28-31

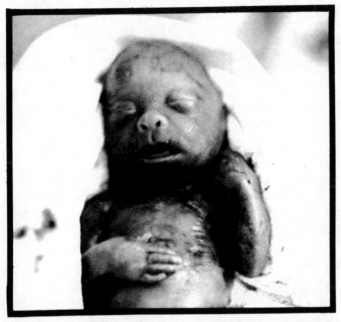

This is a picture of Michael Tim Engelman, born prematurely at 23 weeks, one week before a widely-accepted deadline for therapeutic abortions. Michael's skin appears dark because of respiratory difficulties he experienced during birth.

MINISTRY AVAILABLE

As a consequence of the experiences shared in this book, Phil and Sue Engelman have developed a teaching and singing ministry. You may contact them at (813)347-0661 or (619)325-1770.

FIVE BOOKS COULD SAVE FIVE BABIES!

Did you know that between January 22, 1973 when abortion was legalized in the United States and December 31, 1986, it is estimated that 20 million babies were legally aborted?

As publishers, we have waited years for this book. It speaks powerfully though obliquely to the pro-life issues facing America and Canada. We are persuaded that no girl could ever abort her child after reading this wrenching story.

If you could distribute 5 copies of this book, please clip the coupon below and send it along with your check or money order in U.S. funds to:

> Caring Christians Plan
> Drawer AA
> Cathedral City, CA 92234
> (619)325-1770

NAME _____

ADDRESS _____

_____

(please give street address if possible)

_____ Please ship one shrink-wrap of 5 books of Born Too Soon. I enclose $34.75 in U.S. funds. Postage free.

_____ Please ship one copy of Born Too Soon. I enclose $6.95 plus $1.50 shipping and handling.

(California residents please add 6 percent tax)

And If You'd Like To Do More

You can MAKE A CASE FOR LIFE by giving away a case of life-saving books!

The Caring Christian Plan allows for the purchase of case lots of *Born Too Soon* at half price, provided the books are not for resale. Forty (40) copies at $6.95 represents a retail value of $278. Under the Caring Christians Plan, your cost is $139, plus $15 for shipping and handling, for a total of $154 U.S. funds.

Clip the following coupon and mail along with your check or money order in U.S. funds to:

> Caring Christians Plan
> Drawer AA
> Cathedral City, CA 92234
> Telephone (619)325-1770

NAME _____

ADDRESS _____

_____

(please give street address if possible)

_____ Please find enclosed my check for $154 U.S. funds for a give-away case of *Born Too Soon*.